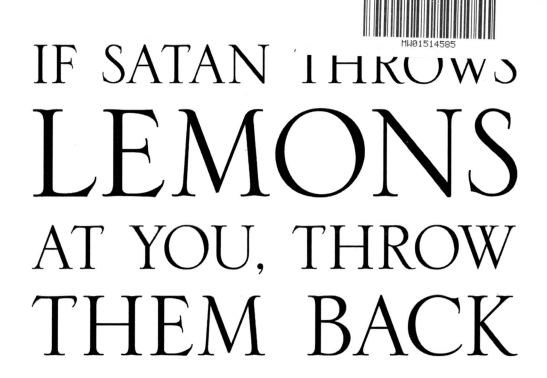

IF SATAN THROWS
LEMONS
AT YOU, THROW
THEM BACK

USING DIFFICULT TIMES TO STRENGTHEN OUR FAITH

ANN VOGEL

WinePressPublishing
Great Books, Defined.

ISBN 13: 978-1-4141-2337-0
ISBN 10: 1-4141-2337-X
Library of Congress Catalog Card Number: 2012905435

Dedicated to Deborah and Andrew Vogel

CONTENTS

Part Three: The "Deadly Sins"

Part Four: The Fruit

Part Five: How Many Lemons Is It Going to Take?

Part Six: Getting Down and Dirty

Part Seven: Something New

ACKNOWLEDGMENTS

Thanks to Deborah Vogel and Nancy Schackman for their assistance in getting this ready to print. I could NOT have done this without you. Thank you for your encouragement as well.

Thank you to the Winepress team for the work and encouragement. Thank you also for finding my manuscript both at a conference and worth working with. You all are my heroes.

INTRODUCTION

I have had enough experiences in my life to know that when things finally seem to be going well or I think I finally have figured out what the Lord wants me to do, sometimes, everything collapses.

Many of us had tough childhoods. Many of us have tough circumstances now. In reality, everyone goes through hard times. The cliché is, "When life gives you lemons, make lemonade," but 99.99 percent of the time, that does not work. Most of the time, the "lemons" cannot be fixed with all the sugar in the world. At such times, we have two choices: either jump in a hole, letting the lemons rot all around us, or run to our heavenly Father and watch what He can make of the lemons and us.

In the Bible, God *never* promises that Christians will not have problems. In fact, the Bible specifically tells us that we will face difficulties; however, it also says that we are not alone and God is in control.

Paul writes, "… all things work together for good … to those who are the called according to His purpose" (Romans 8:28). Exactly what does being "the called according to His purpose" mean in light of the rough times we face? It means that it is our responsibility to discover God's purpose in the trial and make the best of the situation. Doing our best just may mean that we allow the situation to draw us nearer to Him. After all, that is better than letting the situation drive a wedge between the Lord and us. In fact, isn't that just what Satan wants—situations that separate us from God? The Lord promised never to leave us or forsake us (see Hebrews 13:5) and always to walk with us. Those are just two of His many awesome promises to us.

So walk with me through the pages of this book, and learn how to use those lemons to draw closer to God instead of allowing them to make you bitter. It is my desire that you will answer the questions, look up the verses, and prayerfully make this your own study. In addition, I encourage you to keep a prayer journal while you are reading. If you find that you do not have enough room to answer the questions, use your journal or a notebook.

Let me warn you that if you are looking for an easy answer to life's troubles, you won't find it here. If you want to blame God for your troubles, this book will not give you justification to do so. If you are looking for clichés to help you deal with the most difficult times of your life, you won't find them here either.

What will you find? You will find *no* judgment; I have no authority to judge anyone, only the Lord does. You also will see that bad things happen to everyone, even the most devoted Christians. Be reminded that believers have Christ, who overcame this world.

For new Christians (and maybe older ones too), this book describes the source of our faith and how that is pertinent to our keeping strong under pressure. For seeking people, the book is a gentle observation that no one is perfect aside from Christ and that He is with us always.

In addition to all that, you will discover some handy cleaning tips and get to delve a little deeper into the history of the Jewish people. This study includes some Greek and Hebrew translations, practical applications to life, and questions for reflection. It is perfect for individual or group study.

Blessings in your journey!

PART ONE

THOSE BEAUTIFUL LEMON TREES

CHAPTER 1

THE OFFERING SYSTEM

I am definitely not tall or pretty, and because I am a sinner, I do not permeate the air with a wonderful scent unless I accept that because of Christ, I am a sweet-smelling offering to God. That is a deep thought. God said He could not stand the stench of sin, which was one of the reasons for the continuous offerings in the Temple. Then Christ came as the final sacrifice for sin, and His blood covered our sins forever. Thank goodness, because God, His Father, no longer wanted to smell our sins.

Jesus covering and washing away our sins is something like house cleaning. Many cleaning products are lemon-scented, and even though you do not want your company to know you worked so hard to clean the house, the aroma remains. God had the cleaning solution planned from the beginning and used it to cleanse us of our sins. Just as we are proud of our clean homes, God is proud of His Son, and the aroma of the cleansing of Christ remains on us once we accept Jesus and His sacrifice for us. Various scriptures back up this point:

> For we are to God the aroma of Christ among those who are being saved and those who are perishing.
>
> —2 Corinthians 2:15

This is the regular burnt offering instituted at Mount Sinai as a pleasing aroma, an offering made to the Lord by fire.

—Numbers 28:6

I have received full payment and even more; I am amply supplied, now that I have received from Epaphroditus the gifts you sent. They are a fragrant offering, an acceptable sacrifice, pleasing to God.

—Philippians 4:18

Lemon trees are tall and stately, growing ten to twenty feet tall. They cannot handle any cold weather and need irrigation if they get too dry. If the wind blows too hard, they lose their leaves and possibly crops as well. Lemon trees permeate the air with a wonderful aroma, both from their flowers and their oil. However, just like any other beautiful thing in nature, the lemon tree has God-created defense mechanisms. The twigs have thorns, and the juice of the lemon is acidic. This discourages birds and other animals from climbing up the tree or flying by and taking a taste. For them, it is just not worth getting sprayed in the eye with the acidic juice or ending up with a thorn in the beak or paw.

Now let's do a little examination. Here is a list of the offerings commanded in the old covenant:

- The burnt offering was voluntary, covered sins, and symbolized surrender, love, and commitment to God.
- The grain offering was also voluntary and was a way of giving thanks for first fruits—the first of the crops.
- The fellowship or peace offering, also voluntary, symbolized fellowship with God. This offering included:

  a. The thank offering, representing thankfulness for a special blessing.
  b. The vow offering, which offered a ritual expression of a vow.
  c. The freewill offering, symbolizing general thankfulness.

- The sin offering was a mandatory offering with varying degrees of sacrifice based on the economic status of the person giving the offering.
- The guilt offering was another mandatory offering. Someone who either had kept someone from having his or her rights or had desecrated something holy made this offering. Lepers also used it for purification.

The Jewish system was based on holiness, bloodguilt, and blood washing guilt away. The Jewish people feared offending God with any sin and (in most ways) clung to the Law.

When someone sinned or potentially sinned, he or she made a sin offering. This offering was for any sin that a person may not have thought of confessing. Consider the following verses from Leviticus that tell about the sin offering:

> Tell the Israelites: When a person sins unintentionally by straying from any of God's commands, breaking what must not be broken, if it's the anointed priest who sins and so brings guilt on the people, he is to bring a bull without defect to God as an Absolution-Offering for the sin he has committed.
>
> —Leviticus 4:2–3 MSG

> If the whole congregation sins unintentionally by straying from one of the commandments of God that must not be broken, they become guilty even though no one is aware of it. When they do become aware of the sin they've committed, the congregation must bring a bull as an Absolution-Offering and present it at the Tent of Meeting.
>
> —Leviticus 4:13–14 MSG

> When a ruler sins unintentionally by straying from one of the commands of his God, which must not be broken, he is guilty. When he becomes aware of the sin he has committed, he must bring a goat for his offering, a male without any defect, lay his hand on the head of the goat, and slaughter it in the place where they slaughter the Whole-Burnt-Offering in the presence of God—it's an Absolution-Offering.
>
> —Leviticus 4:22–24 MSG

> When an ordinary member of the congregation sins unintentionally, straying from one of the commandments of God, which must not be broken, he is guilty. When he is made aware of his sin, he shall bring a goat, a female without any defect, and offer it for his sin.
>
> —Leviticus 4:27–28 MSG

Each of the offerings, with the exception of the grain and the sin offerings for the very poor, required the blood sacrifice of an unblemished animal. And both those who did sin and those who *might* have sinned needed to make the sin offering. What a Catch-22! A person, at least a person who truly loves God, does not want to be dishonest with Him. So even if a person like that believed he had followed the Law to the letter but thought that perhaps he had slipped up somewhere needed to make a sacrifice. All of the people living under this sacrificial system walked with guilt raining on their shoulders.

Thankfully, we no longer live under such a system. Jesus' blood took care of it all for us. We are still perfectly free to offer God our freewill praise and thanks, but we can do nothing to rid ourselves of our sins. Jesus paid all of that.

Dear sister or brother, I struggled a long time with believing that one thing I had done was just too awful for the Lord to forgive me. Then a wise man told me that God forgave me when

I accepted Christ. He forgave me when I confessed the sin. The man asked me, "What more do you want done to Jesus? Do you want Him flogged more? Spit on more? Beaten more? Crucified again?" Of course, the answer is "no." Jesus' blood covers it all: the past, the present, and the future. The hard part for me, and indeed for some of you, is accepting it. We want to fix it, just like a two-year-old saying, "Me do it," when she knows she can't. We can't cover our own sins either. Only Jesus can.

We treat our problems like lemons, and our lemon trees have thorns. The more we buy into the "me do it" frame of mind, the more the thorns and acidic juice hurt us. We mistakenly think that if we hurt enough and punish ourselves enough, then maybe God will forgive us. How much is going to be enough? We are going about this all wrong.

Questions for Thought

1. Why is it so important that Christ was the final sacrifice for sin, and His blood shed on the cross provided atonement for your sins *once and for all*?

2. Do you struggle with that? How? What else could the Lord have done to cover your sins?

3. How burdensome would you find this offering system if we had to live under it today?

4. Remember, the offering had to be perfect and exchanged for the temple coins. Would you continue to worship at the temple? How? Why would you continue to worship at the temple?

5. Drawing from what you learned in this chapter, what do the following scriptures mean to you? (There is no right or wrong answer.)

- Hebrews 9:14–28

Jesus paid it all and we no longer have to sacrifice bulls and goat to be burned

- Hebrews 10:5–18

No more sacrifice to be made Jesus is our only sacrifice. God did not like those sacrifices

- Ephesians 5:2

Jesus gave himself for us. No more burned offering. God did not like those anyway

6. What are the connections between the old sacrificial system and the new?

Jesus

7. What prophecies or foreshadowing do you notice? Is the New Covenant a hastily made-up plan B, or was it in the original plan all along? Why or why not?

God planed for Jesus to be the offering no more animals on the altar

Nothing that we have done is too terrible for God to forgive. The cross covers everything.

CHAPTER 2

THIS IS JUST TOO HARD

Do you ever think that this Christianity thing is just too hard? We are required to do so many things, like love others and forgive as Christ forgave us. We have a blue print to follow in the New Testament, but it is so hard!

My biggest issue was forgiving my mother. She and I butted heads from the moment I hit puberty, perhaps even before. I could not please her. I was the youngest of her very bright and talented children, so each of my accomplishments was "ho-hum" and expected. Instead of celebrating my endeavors, she found things to criticize about me. All I wanted was her love, and I would have done anything to get it. I jumped through hoop after hoop and could not quite reach my goal of pleasing her. Finally, while I cared for her as she was dying, she told me she had always loved me. All those years, we had not spoken what Gary Smalley in *The Five Love Languages* would call "the same love language." In the end, we forgave each other. We finally opened our hearts and let each other in.

I am sure that the Israelites in Jesus' time had personal problems just as I do, but they also had the sacrificial system to worry about. Then on top of the sacrificial system and the requirements to support the priests, Caesar taxed them from afar in Rome, taking "tribute." In other words, the money sent to Caesar was extortion to keep his armies in check. This tribute was collected as a land tax, a poll tax (this was a kind of "progressive income tax"), and a tax on personal property. If a person lived in Jerusalem, Rome taxed his house. There also were export and import taxes paid at the city gates. Private contractors—hired Israelites—working for the Roman "enemy" performed this "service." As long as the Israelites provided the "service" and the money came in, Rome ignored the profit those private contractors added to the taxes and kept for themselves.

In addition, the people had to pay the temple tax instated by Herod and tithe (10 percent) of what the soil produced. At least this latter tax was somewhat close to the original instructions from the Lord. Still, all of the taxes and offerings were a huge burden on the people.

What if a person sinned and didn't know it? I have not even gone into what made a person "unclean" yet. The Jews cherished going to Jerusalem for the Passover. What if they could not afford all of the various taxes and offerings? The priests inspected the offerings, and funny thing, the priests usually found the people's offerings unacceptable. Therefore, they had to buy the more expensive animals that were onsite. No wonder Jesus exploded when He witnessed this happening in His Father's house. Jesus entered the temple area and drove out all who were buying and selling there. He overturned the tables of the moneychangers and the benches of those selling doves. (The poor could afford to offer doves.) He proclaimed that they had turned the temple into a den of thieves, saying, "It is written … My house will be called a house of prayer, but you are making it a den of robbers" (Matthew 21:12–13 NRSV).

As Jesus was preparing the scourge He used to drive out the moneychangers, no doubt He was thinking about Isaiah 56:7, which says, "These I will bring to my holy mountain and give them joy in my house of prayer. Their burnt offerings and sacrifices will be accepted on my altar; for my house will be called a house of prayer for all nations." Jesus would much rather have seen people in His house who were bringing heart-felt offerings and prayers unhindered by those trying to make a profit.

Anything that profanes God and His house or that gets in the way of people accessing Him infuriates Him. The religious leaders had made the basic Ten Commandments and a few other commands into a complicated system that shut many of God's people out. The Law had morphed into a matter of their being able to turn a lamp on or off on the Sabbath. They concerned themselves with how many steps a person could walk on the Sabbath without "working" instead of with devotion to God. They quibbled about the length of the tassels on men's prayer shawls, which indicated piety, instead of how to behave as God's people. They recognized God, yet still, with their earthly power, they fell into the trap of exclusivity, wanting the entire nation to do things their way. Isaiah 52:5–6 states, "'And now what do I have here?' declares the Lord. 'For my people have been taken away for nothing, and those who rule them mock,' declares the Lord. 'And all day long, my name is constantly blasphemed. Therefore my people will know my name; therefore in that day they will know that it is I who foretold it. Yes, it is I.'"

Questions for Thought

1. When non-believers look at Christians, what do you think they see? How have we made Christianity complicated for them?

2. Do the people around you know that you are a Christian? Why or why not?

   yes, I tell

3. Do you profane God publically or privately in some actions, words, or deeds? (Pray about this one before answering.)

4. Does your church have unspoken "rules" about who can worship there?

   I do not know.

If you are a Christian, Christ lives within you, and He loves you. That love is unconditional. However, His last command was for us to "go into *all the world* and preach the good news to all creation" (Mark 16:15, emphasis mine). Our lives, our churches, and our Bible studies must have the goal of leading others to Him. Write any thoughts you have about this here:

CHAPTER 3

LEFT OUT
IN THE COLD

Our lemon tree cannot handle cold weather. I look at that as "being left out in the cold" or abandoned. Our Father promised that He would never abandon us or leave us out in the cold. Oh, I see you, shaking your head. I've been there too. There definitely were times when I felt God had left me all alone. However, there comes a time when even wounded hearts have to step out in faith.

Jesus specialized in healing while He was on Earth. He was showing us what His Father is like. I admit that I get very frightened when the Lord tells me to do things like expose myself as I'm doing in this book. But He is the perfect Father, and one must start trusting sometime. We must trust that He will be with us even when we are afraid. Hebrews 13:5 says, "Keep your lives free from the love of money and be content with what you have, because God has said, 'Never will I leave you; never will I forsake you.'"

Matthew 6:8 (NLT) tells us, "Do not be like them, for your Father knows what you need before you ask him." Matthew referred to the priests who stood in the streets or in the synagogues praying. At that time, people, mostly the priests, prayed in the streets. Jesus questioned their motives. If we read Scripture in context, the instruction is to speak directly to the Father, without fanfare. God is our Father; we do not need to have an audience. We do not need to convince others of our Christian vocabulary or biblical knowledge. God is our Father; He knows what we need, and He is waiting for us to ask Him for help. He may not answer immediately or in the way we expect. He is God.

Also, when we pray, we need to begin by acknowledging who our Father is, not just rush to our laundry list of requests. Prayer is a conversation. Next, we need to acknowledge our sins and take responsibility for them. In our society, taking responsibility, especially for wrongdoing, is rare. Yet, our Father demands that we confess that we have done things that disappoint Him. We all do. He will forgive us for our sins, if we have accepted Jesus as our Savior, because Jesus took our punishment on the cross.

Romans 3:22–24 (NIV) says, "This righteousness from God comes through faith in Jesus Christ to all who believe. There is no difference, for all have sinned and fall short of the glory of God, and are justified freely by his grace through the redemption that came by Christ Jesus."

I know what you are thinking. *But it's cold. My leaves are falling off. I am naked, and I'm dying inside.* Trust this truth: Jesus has been there. Jesus has been cold. He has been naked, or near to it, on the cross, and His friends left Him. Even His Father turned His face away for a time.

Still your insides are screaming, *But I have asked and asked, begged and pleaded, and all I got was a big fat "NO."*

This is where our faith comes in. Re-read Matthew 6:8. Our Father knows what we need. We don't always know what we need, but we sure know what we want, and we want it *now*! Regardless of that, I have found that God has been right every time He denied my requests. His timing is always the best timing. If I run ahead of Him, I trip.

Romans 8:15 says, "For you did not receive a spirit that makes you a slave again to fear, but you received the Spirit of sonship. And by Him we cry, 'Abba, Father.'" The key is running to Daddy. Run to "Abba." Nowhere does it say that we have to understand or that God must explain Himself to us. Sometime in the future, He might ask us to use the experience, but when the experience comes, don't run away.

It was difficult for me to think of God as my daddy. That idea conjured up thoughts of a father who was never there, who didn't support me, etc. I did not want a father. Then someone told me to think of and write down the aspects of a perfect father. I did, and the heavenly Father fit everything I wrote on my list. Now I run to Him during the times I need Him, and He is always there. He may not "fix" things when I want Him to, but He never leaves me to deal with things alone.

"Abba" God is the perfect Father. While Jesus walked among us, He and His Father were not just spiritual, unemotional figureheads. They loved each other just as human parents and children love each other. They kept their connection, and Jesus was not alone until He had the weight of all the sins of the world on His shoulders. Then His Father had to turn away; God's holiness and our sin cannot dwell together.

God and His Son love each other with the deep love that only exists between parents and their children. God desires for us to experience this same kind of loving relationship with Him.

God desires a relationship with us, not religion. What's the difference? Religion is about rules. Relationships are about love. The disciple John says it best in the following verses:

> My dear children, I am writing this to you so that you will not sin. But if anyone does sin, we have an advocate who pleads our case before the Father. He is Jesus Christ, the one who is truly righteous.
>
> He himself is the sacrifice that atones for our sins—and not only our sins but the sins of all the world. And we can be sure that we know him if we obey his commandments. If someone claims, "I know God," but doesn't obey God's commandments, that person is a liar and is not living in the truth. But those who obey God's word truly show how completely they love him. That is how we know we are living in him. Those who say they live in God should live their lives as Jesus did.
>
> —1 John 2:1–6 NLT

> But if we confess our sins to him, he is faithful and just to forgive us our sins and to cleanse us from all wickedness.
>
> —1 John 1:9 NLT

Questions for Thought

1. What part of you needs healing? *Thought, even though I know for a fact Jesus died for me.*

2. Is it problematic for you to see God as your heavenly Father? Why? *not as much as it used to.*

3. How would you describe a perfect father? *Some one I did not need to be afraid of. I was very afraid of my own dad.*

4. When do you feel like you are shivering in the cold? Do you feel like God is with you during those times? Why or why not?

5. Pray and ask the Lord what is blocking you from doing what He wants you to do. Are there bad memories? To answer this question, it may be beneficial for you to get help from a qualified Christian brother or sister.

6. What is it that you need spiritually?

God sent His only Son to die for our sins. If we accept that, confess our sins, and follow Him, we are saved from the consequences of our sins. We now have an amazing relationship with Jesus. We can speak to Him, cry with Him, and laugh with Him because He understands what it is like to be human. The only "rule" is that you have to accept Christ into your heart. He will direct you from there. *Listen to Him.*

Write a prayer here:

CHAPTER 4

ASKING GOD FOR HELP

One of my biggest challenges, now that I have multiple sclerosis, is asking for help. I was a registered nurse, the caregiver, and I never had to ask for help from anyone. Well, times have changed. Not only do I have to rely on the Lord now, but also I must rely on others to help me. The sad part is that it took that diagnosis to teach me, even though I am a Christian, that I must rely on God and others. I must open up to others. I have to ask for help.

It is ironic that in order to plant a lemon tree, a person has to dig the hole a little bit less than the height of the root system and at least twice as wide. With the tree standing straight, the root system needs to be slightly exposed when the gardener places the tree in the hole. Then the gardener may refill the hole with soil, pressing it down well to remove the air pockets. The gardener needs to water the tree deeply and spread a layer of compost to keep the moisture in; however, the mulch cannot touch the trunk of the tree, because it can cause the trunk to rot. It is important to water the tree weekly until the water penetrates to the roots.

One key thing I noted after learning about planting a lemon tree was this: the tree needed a really big hole! When one digs a hole for a lemon tree, he or she digs with a specific purpose and for the tree's benefit. If God, our Gardener, is planting us where He wants us, we, like a lemon tree, will have to endure those purposeful holes until our roots are set as they should be. However, how often do we dig ourselves into huge pits, find that we cannot get out on our own, and then yell to God for help?

This reminds me of Joseph. Joseph was the apple of his father Jacob's eye, and neither Jacob nor Joseph tried to hide that fact. Jacob made a special coat for his youngest son. Obviously, then Joseph's other brothers were jealous. Matters were only made worse when Joseph tattled on them and told his brothers of dreams he had that showed how, in the future, they would bow down and serve him (Genesis 37:2–10).

One day, their jealousy boiled over, and the brothers threw Joseph into a pit. At first they were going kill him, but his brother Reuben convinced the others to throw Joseph in a well instead. He wanted to return and rescue Joseph.

A little later, Judah, another brother, saw a caravan approaching and realized that they could make a profit with their brother. When Reuben returned to the well, Joseph had vanished. I suppose one could make the argument that Joseph had dug this pit for himself and he needed God's help to free him. However, we will find that Joseph's pit eventually led him to the palace.

Joseph's brothers sold him to slavers who were Midianites/Ishmaelites for twenty pieces of silver. The Midianites traveled the trade routes and took Joseph into Egypt. His brothers took his distinctive coat, bloodied it up, and they told their father wild animals killed Joseph. The problem was that God saw what the brothers did. Joseph's story is a soap opera, complete with intrigue, but it is abundantly clear that Joseph was God's man.

Joseph started out in Egypt as a slave to Potiphar. Potiphar held a position as a high official in Pharaoh's house. For Joseph, this was an opportunity, but he did not know it. His job with Potiphar began Joseph's climb to power in Pharaoh's house. Joseph stood out among Potiphar's slaves. He did not bow down to pressure, and he did not bow down to other gods, including Pharaoh.

Pharaoh, along with the prior and future Pharaohs, believed he held human powers as the son of Ra, the sun god, or the incarnation of Horus, the god of war. Pharaohs were named after "Atum Ra" after the first Ra, who, according to their beliefs, grew tired, kissed his family good-bye, and created the first mound (Iunu) to rise from the waters of Nun. Shu and Tefnut gave birth to the earth (Geb) and the sky (Nut), who gave birth to Osiris, Isis, Set, Nephthys, and Horus the elder.[1]

The real God, whom Joseph worshipped, protected him. Joseph set himself apart. He worshipped his God, did not eat unclean food, and did not hide it. (This was risky in a land where people worshipped their leader as god.) Everyone knew Joseph was an honest man.

Unfortunately, Joseph was young and handsome, and he caught the eye of his master's wife. Potiphar's wife thought that Joseph could keep her company during her lonely days. Joseph was not naïve and refused. Joseph refused to make a fool of his master and, more than that, to sin against God. So Potiphar's wife accused Joseph of rape. Then Joseph, despite his reputation, was imprisoned.

Through some amazing turns of events, Joseph wound up interpreting Pharaoh's disturbing dreams that were actually warnings of a coming famine. There would be seven years of plentiful harvests and then seven years of severe drought and famine. Pharaoh rewarded Joseph for interpreting the dreams by putting him in charge of the next fourteen years.

The seven good years happened, and the Egyptians saved half of the land's yield. The seven bad years came as well, and because of Joseph's shrewd organization, the entire known world affected by the famine came to Egypt for help, including Joseph's brothers. When Joseph saw his brothers, he recognized them immediately, but they did not recognize him. Probably the last thing the brothers were expecting was to meet up with the brother they figured was dead.

Before they left for home, Joseph put a silver cup in his youngest brother's bag. Then he let them get out of the gates and sent the guards after them. He meant to hold the youngest boy, Benjamin, "hostage" until his father and the rest of the family came. Yet Judah appealed to Joseph, asking Joseph to allow him to stay in Benjamin's place. Judah knew his father loved Benjamin deeply and could not stand another loss.

Eventually, after having his brothers jump through a few hoops so he could see if they had changed, Joseph revealed himself to his brothers, assisted his family with food, and eventually, moved them all to the best land in Egypt. Joseph told his brothers, "Don't you see, you planned evil against me but God used those same plans for my good, as you see all around you right now—life for many people" (Genesis 50:20 MSG).

Asking for help is not a bad thing, but pride is. Not trusting God is also a bad thing. Jacob had dug himself a deep hole by showing favoritism. Then Joseph's brothers did the same thing through their sins of jealousy, covetousness, and bitterness. However, seeing how Joseph emerged from his pit to serve in Egypt as the person who was second only to Pharaoh proves that God is stronger than any pit, even though God's purpose may include the pit for a brief time. (You can read the full story of Joseph in Genesis 37–50.)

> But do not forget this one thing, dear friends: With the Lord a day is like a thousand years, and a thousand years are like a day.
>
> —2 Peter 3:8

Questions for Thought

1. Why do you think Jacob's sons had the characteristics of jealousy, covetousness, and bitterness? Do you have some of those characteristics?

2. Do you see how God was in control of Joseph's entire situation? How was He in control?

3. Going back to our illustration of planting the lemon tree, in the situation with Joseph and his brothers (make sure you read the Bible chapters about Joseph—Genesis 37–47):

    a. What kind of water did God use?

    b. What compost did God use to help Joseph stand?

4. What is the lesson here?

5. We also have to stand straight before God, even though others may think that He is not watching. Joseph was true to his beliefs. Are you true to your beliefs when no one is watching?

    We need to trust God, even when we are in the "pit." I know it is not easy, but if we drink deeply from the well of living water, we might actually learn a few things along the way. I know I have.

    This lesson may speak to you differently. Write the lesson you learned here:

CHAPTER 5

GROUND YOURSELF IN THE WORD

Until I personally started studying the Scriptures, I was content simply to listen to what the minister said. I did not become a Christian until just before I got married, and then a new world opened up to me as I attended women's and couples' Bible studies at church. Because I was learning to study God's Word, when I ended up on bed rest with one pregnancy, I was able to delve into the Gospels. I plunged my new roots into the ground. It was a frightening time as far as the pregnancy was concerned, but it was a wonderful time of spiritual growth. I actually studied the Bible using commentaries and dictionaries. I had never before learned so much at one time!

Lemon trees have wide root systems; they may push out thirty to forty feet from the canopy of the tree. Their root balls weigh about 500–600 pounds, and the soil surrounding them must be porous. If someone uproots and moves an older tree, it most likely will not survive the shock to its system. In addition, lemon trees don't tolerate drought, so gardeners need to water them at least twice a week if it doesn't rain.

So how does this apply to us? Our "roots" lie in the Old Testament, all the way back to Genesis, all the way back to the Garden of Eden. Genesis 3:2–7 says:

> The woman said to the serpent, "We may eat fruit from the trees in the garden, but God did say, 'You must not eat fruit from the tree that is in the middle of the garden, and you must not touch it, or you will die.'"

"You will not surely die," the serpent said to the woman. "For God knows that when you eat of it your eyes will be opened, and you will be like God, knowing good and evil." When the woman saw that the fruit of the tree was good for food and pleasing to the eye, and also desirable for gaining wisdom, she took some and ate it. She also gave some to her husband, who was with her, and he ate it. Then the eyes of both of them were opened, and they realized they were naked; so they sewed fig leaves together and made coverings for themselves.

From this scripture, we know that Satan deceived Adam and Eve into breaking the one rule God gave them: do not touch or eat that fruit. Satan taunted them by appealing to their pride. In essence, the old snake was saying, "Well, He just does not want you to be like Him." Satan does this frequently; he uses our pride against us. Pride is a sore point with many of us. Adam and Eve should have known that they couldn't be like the Almighty God! He is the Creator ... their Creator. But power is seductive.

Despite their sin, God did not give up on them. Yes, He threw them out of the garden. Yes, they had to work for a living. Yes, women now have to bear children in pain. And yes, people die, but it could have been worse. God still loved them, and He set a plan in motion to redeem them. Genesis 3:15 reads, "And I will put enmity between you and the woman, and between your offspring and hers; he will crush your head, and you will strike his heel." (God says this to Satan after Adam and Eve's plunge into sin.) This was a foreshadowing of what Jesus would do through His death and resurrection to redeem man.

Even though God eventually had to start the human race over with Noah, His great love for man remained intact. God still loves His children. He carries them and keeps His promises to them.

Mark 7:21–23 says, "For from within, out of the heart of man, come evil thoughts, sexual immorality, theft, murder, adultery, coveting, wickedness, deceit, sensuality, envy, slander, *pride*, foolishness. All these evil things come from within, and they defile a person" (ESV, emphasis mine). I guess we cannot say, "The devil made me do it."

Pride is seductive. It entices us. We all want others to recognize us for our hard work, don't we? We think, *It is only right.* I was proud of my intellect and independence before the doctor diagnosed me with MS. I was proud of how I studied the Scriptures, proud of my church participation, and proud of how I taught my children. Then I had to realize that my only source of pride should come through Christ and what He did and does through me.

Pride is to "show oneself," to hold your head high, even over God's head. We don't deserve to be proud about anything. *Everything* we have comes from God. We can't be like God so we need not break our arms patting ourselves on the back! We need to get rid of the "little gods" in our lives. Remember the history of the Israelites that the Bible records. In it, we see the consistency of God's people; they kept sliding away and drawing close, sliding away and drawing close. Yet through it all, God continued loving them, but He also became angrier and angrier.

The pit of pride is dangerous. It is a huge temptation to fall into. The only one who can help us is Christ, who actually has the right to be proud. Philippians 2:7–8 says, "But made himself nothing, taking the very nature of a servant … he humbled himself and became obedient to death—even death on a cross!" The Son of God, Creator, King, Redeemer, and Lord are His names; yet He was meek and chose self-denial instead of self-promotion.[2]

Jesus chose to come to earth as a helpless baby. His parents raised him like any other Jewish boy. Yet, when He knew the time was right, He left and prepared for ministry. We need to remember that Jesus could say "no" at any time. He knew His Father's plan. Think of how much love He had, how much love this required. There was no room for pride, no room to impress others with His powers; that is what the temptation in the desert was about (Matthew 4:1–11). Jesus knew that if He caved into Satan's temptations, the plan was over. Satan would remain in control. Yet, Jesus replied with Scripture from the "Old Testament" (there was no "New Testament" yet). This is our model: use Scripture. Remember, our pride only comes from who we are in Christ.

Think of that, the King, the King of Kings, choosing to be meek, following His Father's will, choosing to love His people without proclaiming who He is in a grand manner. He spoke with a quiet, "Follow me."

Even if we grew up in the church, we must remember that no one is perfect, no one is better than God is, and everyone needs Christ. The roots laid down in the Old Testament formed the basis for the towering tree that is the New Testament. It is a beautiful thing.

Questions for Thought

1. Why is it a good idea to study both the Old and New Testaments?

2. Lemon trees require frequent watering. How does this translate to your life?

3. Why would it be bad if Adam and Eve were like God?

4. What are your points of pride? *my voice, my hair*

5. What are your little gods? *T, V,*

Before MS, I was proud of my intellectual abilities. The diagnosis was a relief because no one knew the source of my problems. Some thought I was hysterical or depressed. I associated MS with mobility problems, even though I am an R.N. What can I say? School was a long time ago! But some of the symptoms I listed included odd brain functioning and seizures. I cannot drive, and I cannot work as a nurse anymore.

My source of pride is my intellect, but MS is slowly robbing me of that. I will lose and am losing the other things people associate with MS, but that did not bother me until I realized that someone eventually would have to help me. That was another blow to my pride. Yes, I have assistive devices and a service dog, and for now, I can still write, but I have to rely on God for the ability to do so many things, especially communicating the message that He wants me to deliver. I have nothing to be proud of. Frankly, I stay in control only by relying on God; the deeper I am in His Word, the easier it is to rely on Him.

You have to rely on God as well. Thankfully, you do not need a chronic illness to rely on God. In 1 John 4:15–16, God promises, "If anyone acknowledges that Jesus is the Son of God, God lives in him and he in God. And so we know and rely on the love God has for us." Rely on Jesus, and stay in the Word.

CHAPTER 6

A PLEASING AROMA

An equal amount of lemon juice and water added to an atomizer will create a wonderful, synthetic, chemical-free, and green air freshener for your home—a pleasing aroma. I think I read that somewhere before. Therefore, I guess that the lemons in my life can be offered up to God as a pleasing aroma too.

It is time for a little history lesson. Jews believe that their offerings are a pleasing aroma to God and not just a pay-off for sin. To them, Yahweh's greatness and what He did for His people are embodied in the sacrificial system. After the destruction of the temple in Jerusalem, in 70 A.D., Rome legislated that sacrifices outside a temple were illegal. The Jews associated the destruction of the temple with the coming of the Messiah.[10]

Genesis 49:10 (MSG) states, "The scepter shall not leave Judah; He'll keep a firm grip on the command staff. Until the ultimate ruler comes and the nations obey him." The Jews believed that this scripture stated that the Messiah would come in the first century and before the tribe of Judah lost its identity as a people. The temple was not just a building to the Jews. People could only make their offerings at the temple. It was the center of learning and social life. God resided in the Holy of Holies. Without the temple, God did not have a presence in Judah, so they thought that if the temple was gone, the Messiah was on His way! The problem was that the Messiah had to meet their expectations despite any circumstances.[10]

Obedience was the other issue plaguing the Jews from the beginning of their relationship with God. God needed to lead them in all their ways, and His people needed to follow Him. It was as simple as that.

When Jews celebrate the Passover, a lamb is partially roasted and partially boiled. Then, according to Leviticus 17:6, "The priest shall throw the blood on the altar of the Lord at the entrance of the tent of meeting and burn the fat for a pleasing aroma to the Lord" (ESV). When the Jews first celebrated the Passover in Egypt, right before the exodus, the markings on the doorposts with a swash of blood on the top and one on either side of the frame identified the homes of God's people during the plague of death. This was a foreshadowing of the cross. Jesus is the Lamb of God, who takes away the sins of the world (John 1:29). He is the paschal lamb indeed, and His sacrifice was a sweet-smelling savor to God. The paschal lamb is the Passover lamb, offered as a remembrance of the Hebrews' rescue from Egypt during the Exodus from Egypt (Exodus 12).

While Jesus was alive on earth, He expected His disciples (the Jewish ones) to continue to observe the Sabbath and carry out the sacrifices, including the Passover. Jesus' crucifixion took place over the Passover weekend. That is why there was such a hurry to try to convict Him. People filled Jerusalem to celebrate the Holy Day. The Jewish leaders and the Romans feared riots. They tried Jesus the night before Passover (illegally) and crucified Him the following morning.

Jesus was the perfect lamb, sinless and obedient. However, Jesus bore the scars of sin, the scourge, the thorned crown, and the nails of the cross. Physically, He could not be a "perfect lamb." The lamb a Jewish family sacrificed had to be without any infirmity, mark, or blemish. The lamb lived with the family for four days. The animal was only a year old, if that. The lamb had to be the healthiest, most playful, and "cute" of the herd. As the lamb lived with the family, in the house, the lamb drew the children to it like a pet. Perhaps the little animal won the affections of the adults as well. Imagine the wailing as the animal was sacrificed and the blood was posted over the door in the following fashion, without the protruding top. Does this remind you of anything?

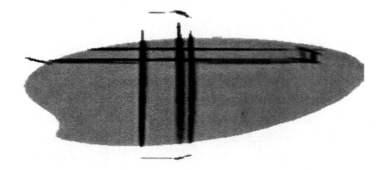

Jesus bore many marks from the scourging and beatings. However, because He was the perfect, sinless Lamb of God, He was able to be the perfect, final sacrifice for sins. Romans 4:25 (NLT) says, "He was handed over to die because of our sins, and he was raised to life to make us right with God."

Hebrews 1:8–9 says that God the Father says to His Son, Jesus, "You're God, and on the throne for good; your rule makes everything right. You love it when things are right; you hate it when things are wrong. That is why God, your God, poured fragrant oil on your head, marking you out as king, far above your dear companions" (MSG).

Ezekiel 20:41 says, "As a pleasing aroma I will accept you, when I bring you out from the peoples and gather you out of the countries where you have been scattered. And I will manifest my holiness among you in the sight of the nations" (ESV). This scripture is from the exile, after God's people forsook Him for gods made of clay and stone. The exile was a parental time-out for His children who had gone astray and become prodigals. This straying to other gods was not just a one-time occurrence. Worshipping other gods continued to be a problem for God's people. They seemed to have a flavor of the month when it came to worship. Almost as soon as they became familiar with people who worshiped some other god, they wanted to do so as well. Finally, God had had enough. Their sacrifices to Him meant nothing, their actions toward Him meant nothing, and their calling as a people reserved for Him meant nothing to them. They continued with the temple worship, burning incense and sacrificing, because it was financially profitable for the business of the temple, but their hearts were not in it. The aroma was not pleasing to God, and He sent them into exile. However, as He promised, He finally gathered them in and forgave them.

Holy means "set apart" or sanctified. When we apply this word to humans, it means a deeply held principle, one coming from the heart. It stems from the part of us that believes that something is the "right thing to do." When used in reference to God, *holiness* means that He is set apart from all, and even with His mercy in drawing us to Himself, [10] He is who He is. God is perfect. God never changes. God is love, and that love never changes. God forgives. He has set in place, through His Son, a means for His people to obtain forgiveness. This is why He calls His children to be different, set apart, holy. *Holy* sounds like a scary word. However, broken down, it simply means we are supposed to be set apart and dedicate our lives to the Lord. The best part is that if we make an error, we have confession and forgiveness.

He was handed over to die because of our sins, and he was raised to life to make us right with God.

—Romans 4:25 NLT

The high and lofty one who lives in eternity, the Holy One, says this: "I live in the high and holy place with those whose spirits are contrite and humble. I restore the crushed spirit of the humble and revive the courage of those with repentant hearts.

—Isaiah 57:15 NLT

Make them holy by your truth; teach them your word, which is truth. Just as you sent me into the world, I am sending them into the world. And I give myself as a holy sacrifice for them so they can be made holy by your truth.

—John 17:17–19 NLT

(Jesus went on to pray for future believers in John 17:17–24.)

Just as God wanted the Israelites' hearts to be in their sacrifices, God wants our hearts to be included in our worship of Him. God desires us to be wholly and truly devoted to Him; He does not desire mechanical attendance. Yes, we may attend services on Sunday or Saturday, but are our hearts in our worship? Do we listen to the teaching?

If Jesus is the Son and He calls us His brothers and sisters, Jesus is our "big brother." Matthew 12:50 (MSG) states, "Obedience is thicker than blood. The person who obeys my heavenly Father's will is my brother and sister and mother." I love my older brothers. They protected me (yes, they teased me as well), supported me, and loved me. Yet, Jesus is able to do this to the extreme. He gave His life for me. He guides me. He never leaves me. Hebrews 13:5 (NRSV) says, "Keep your lives free from the love of money, and be content with what you have; for he has said, 'I will never leave you or forsake you.'"

Questions for Thought

1. Are there some dirty and not-quite-ready places within your life—places that make you feel uncomfortable giving sacrifices to the Lord?

2. Why do you think you feel this way?

3. How do you feel having Jesus Christ as the ultimate big brother? What is important about knowing that Jesus is your big brother? (Hint: If you had a big brother, think about the times that he checked out your dates or took care of you you.)

4. God accepts us. He loves us. We are protected by His blood. We can offer the lemons in our lives up for Him to use, and believe me, He will. What lemons can you offer up to God today?

5. How can/does He show His holiness through you?

The thought that God loves me and accepts me through His Son literally blows me away. My original belief that I could *earn* salvation was wrong. I cannot do *anything* to earn God's grace. I just need to accept the gift. It is a hard concept for someone of my background and independent spirit. Yet, I now understand that I never can be good enough on my own to deserve God's forgiveness. That holds true for all of us.

Part Two

The Lemon Juicer

CHAPTER 7

LEMON JUICE

My mother had an old-school citrus juicer. The thing was huge, about a foot tall, and bright orange. She would cut an orange or a lemon in half, place it rind side up in the juicer, and close the top. Then she would have to press really hard on the handle to extract the juice from the fruit. Sometimes she would press down on the handle two or three times, until she was satisfied that she had squeezed every drop out of the fruit. Then she'd remove the poor rind, all shriveled and barren, and save it in the refrigerator for use in some amazing recipe.

Don't you sometimes feel that you have been put through a juicer? Maybe you don't know exactly who is pushing the handle down, but you do know there isn't any more juice left in you. You are drained, shriveled, and used up. If one more person calls your name, you just might run screaming down the street.

But wait a minute. The truth is that just as my mother never used the juicer without a reason, the Lord never permits pressures to enter our lives without reasons. Sometimes we don't understand exactly why, but these in-the-juicer times can be used for our good and God's glory.

Do you know that lemon juice can be used as a meat tenderizer? Think about that. Sometimes the hard times push us back into the Word and often back into the very lap of our Father. Our hearts can get pretty hard as we face the demands of the house, the family, and the never-ending routine. We may have our quiet times, but are they times of true communication with God or just another part of our routines? The bitter times and sour times are the lemon juice that force us back to our Daddy. Then we speak to Him with our hearts and find that the lemon juice has made us tender and sincere. We are more aware of our pain, and later, because of what we've been through, we become more aware of and compassionate about the pain of others.

Consider Psalms 103:1–22 (MSG):

O my soul, bless GOD. From head to toe, I'll bless his holy name! O my soul, bless GOD, don't forget a single blessing! He forgives your sins—every single one. He heals your diseases—every one. He redeems you from hell—saves your life! He crowns you with love and mercy—a paradise crown. He wraps you in goodness—beauty eternal. He renews your youth—you're always young in his presence. GOD makes everything come out right; he puts victims back on their feet. He showed Moses how he went about his work, opened up his plans to all Israel. GOD is sheer mercy and grace; not easily angered, he's rich in love. He doesn't endlessly nag and scold, nor hold grudges forever. He doesn't treat us as our sins deserve, nor pay us back in full for our wrongs. As high as heaven is over the earth, so strong is his love to those who fear him. And as far as sunrise is from sunset, he has separated us from our sins. As parents feel for their children, GOD feels for those who fear him. He knows us inside and out, keeps in mind that we're made of mud. Men and women don't live very long; like wildflowers they spring up and blossom, But a storm snuffs them out just as quickly, leaving nothing to show they were here. GOD's love, though, is ever and always, eternally present to all who fear him, Making everything right for them and their children as they follow his Covenant ways and remember to do whatever he said. GOD has set his throne in heaven; he rules over us all. He's the King! So bless GOD, you angels, ready and able to fly at his bidding, quick to hear and do what he says. Bless GOD, all you armies of angels, alert to respond to whatever he wills. Bless GOD, all creatures, wherever you are—everything and everyone made by GOD. And you, O my soul, bless GOD!

Rocky times are just a part of life. But perhaps after lemon juice periods of our lives we are more aware of how the Lord provided for us. Or perhaps we are more aware of things in our lives that we need to change. Sometimes, we just need to buckle our seat belts, hold on to Daddy's hand, and trust Him. When we do this, as a result, His purpose is accomplished and our hearts become more tender.

However, what happens when the lemon juicer seems more like a meat grinder? Those are the times when we feel like our world is out of control. We forget that we are not the ones who are in control; God is. That is for a good reason. Romans 8:28–30 (NLT) states, "And we know that God causes everything to work together for the good of those who love God and are called according to his purpose for them. For God knew his people in advance, and he chose them to become like his Son, so that his Son would be the firstborn among many brothers and sisters. And having chosen them, he called them to come to him. And having called them, he gave them right standing with himself. And having given them right standing, he gave them his glory."

When we are grinding our way through the day, it is almost impossible to remember that scripture. Instead, we complain, "So much for quitting smoking, or this diet; I cannot take it anymore." Or we say, "If one more thing happens, I will scream." Not everything that occurs in our lives is good. Evil is here on earth. Yet, God can use tough circumstances for our future good. The purpose is not our happiness; the purpose is God's will. The promise in Romans 8:28–30 is for Christians who chose to trust Christ and His Father. The goal is to become more like Christ as we study the Word, study Jesus' life on earth, pray, accept His Spirit, and work as He did in our world. Through it all, our "treasure" must remain in heaven. Our faith must remain strong in the face of the worst of circumstances. Our purpose is to serve and honor God. After all, He knew you before you were born! Jeremiah 1:5 says, "Before I formed you in the womb I knew you, before you were born I set you apart ..."

You are invited to the great party at the end of the world. Do not miss it! John 5:26 (NLT) says, "The Father has life in himself, and he has granted that same life-giving power to his Son." Romans 11:33–36 (NLT) states, "Oh, how great are God's riches and wisdom and knowledge! How impossible it is for us to understand his decisions and his ways! For who can know the Lord's thoughts? Who knows enough to give him advice? And who has given him so much that he needs to pay it back? For everything comes from him and exists by his power and is intended for his glory. All glory to him forever! Amen."

We need to remember what a mighty God we serve. I know how syrupy that sounds. That is a fancy way of saying trust the Lord. I know it is hard. Trusting is not a strong point of mine. However, in the Christian life, we must learn to trust, and yes, lean on the Lord. First John 4:15–16 (NLT) says, "All who confess that Jesus is the Son of God have God living in them, and they live in God. We know how much God loves us, and we have put our trust in his love. God is love, and all who live in love live in God, and God lives in them." This should not be such a struggle for me, or others. Yet it is. The "trust issue" will always lurk in the background for me. I know the Lord knows me and loves me anyway. He knows the reasons. He knows that I am working on it. I have seen Him work wonders in front of my eyes.

D. L. Moody, of England, sailed to Boston in 1854. At the time, he was a Unitarian. Once he arrived in Boston, he was employed by his uncle to work in a shoe shop. One of the conditions of Moody's employment was that he had to attend Mount Vernon Congregational Church, which was pastored by Reverend Kirk.

One day, Kimball, a Sunday school teacher from Moody's church, found him in the shoe store, wrapping shoes. (Hey, a man has to work!) Kimball shared the gospel with Moody, saying, "I want to tell you how much Christ loves you."

After talking with Kimball, Moody knelt down and was converted. Later, he explained how he felt: "I was in a new world. The birds sang sweeter, the sun shone brighter. I'd never known such peace."[1]

Soon after Moody moved to Chicago in 1856, a revival swept the nation. It lasted until 1859. In Chicago, another of Moody's uncles helped him to get a job in shoe store. During his time there, Moody attended the Plymouth Congregational Church. He also found a tiny Sunday school on the corner of Chicago and Wells streets and helped that class to grow until there were more students than the space could hold.

In 1858, Moody started teaching in an abandoned freight car and then in an abandoned saloon, which he lit with candles. He also spent time in Michigan, teaching children. His school in Chicago eventually grew to the point that the former mayor of Chicago gave Moody the city's north market to use (rent free). Moody gave this to a good friend named Fawell to superintend. The school reached 1,500 children each week.

In 1860, Moody decided to go into ministry full time. In November of that year, President-elect Lincoln visited Moody's Sunday school. Moody took on missionary work for the YMCA in 1861. (When the YMCA grew, Moody became president and served from 1866–1869). Then in 1862, he married, and he and his wife eventually had three children.

During the Civil War, Moody put himself at risk and personally ministered to injured soldiers. He always asked them, "Are you saved?"[2]

Moody continued to teach in his Sunday school and eventually was asked to begin a church. Thus, the Illinois Street Church, now known as Moody church, started in February of 1867. Moody preached until pastor Harwood arrived. Then he supervised the construction of Farwell Hall in and then started his first revival in Philadelphia.

In 1867, Moody sailed to England, partly to relieve his wife's asthma and partly because he wanted to meet two other prominent revival preachers: Charles Spurgeon and George Mueller. Spurgeon was England's best-known preacher of that time-period. He preached Christ only, a subject not popular at the time. Mueller preached faith by Christ alone. His ministry was to orphans, and he relied on Christ alone.

Three important events influenced Moody's decision to become a world evangelist. The first, in 1868, was with another famous preacher named Moorehouse. He told Moody, "Teach what the Bible says, not your own words, and show people how much God loves them." The second was when a man who had attended an Indianapolis YMCA convention joined Moody's ministry in Chicago. The third was the Chicago Fire, which destroyed Moody's church. The church re-opened on December 24, 1871, but Moody was not the pastor because he felt directed to begin a series of crusades across the country. He did so, with huge success. Moody also went on to open schools for both men and women.

Moody had a few "juicer" moments, but not to the extent of his friends. Instead, it seemed that he was blessed with everything he needed. Still, even in tough times, like when his church burnt to the ground, Moody did not give up. His faith carried him to great ministry.

My favorite hymn is "It is Well With My Soul." This hymn was written by one of D.L. Moody's friends, Horatio G. Spafford. Spafford had his share of in-the-juicer times. He lost his son to scarlet fever in 1870, the family home burned down in 1871, and his real estate holdings burned in the Chicago fire. After that, he planned to sail to England with his wife, Anna, and four daughters, but for some reason, Spafford had to stay behind. He decided to send the rest of his family on to England.

On November 2, 1873, the Ville de Havre, the ship on which the Spafford family was sailing, collided with The Lochearn, an English vessel. The ship transporting the family sank in only twelve minutes, claiming the lives of 226 people. Anna Spafford stood bravely on the deck with her daughters, Annie, Maggie, Bessie, and Tanetta, clinging desperately to her. Her last memory was of her baby being torn violently from her arms by the force of the waters. Anna was only saved from the fate of her daughters by a plank that floated beneath her unconscious body, propping her up.

When the survivors of the wreck were rescued and Anna learned that her daughters had not survived, her first reaction was one of complete despair. Then she heard a voice speak to her, saying, *You were spared for a purpose.* She immediately recalled the words of a friend: "It's easy to be grateful and good when you have so much, but take care that you are not a fair-weather friend to God."

Spafford received a telegram from his wife, which only said, "Saved Alone." Upon hearing the terrible news, Horatio Spafford boarded the next ship out of New York to join his bereaved wife. Bertha Spafford—Horatio and Anna's fifth daughter, who was born later—explained that during her father's voyage, the captain of the ship called him to the bridge. He said, "A careful reckoning has been made, and I believe we are now passing the place where the de Havre was wrecked. The water is three miles deep."

Spafford returned to his cabin and penned the lyrics of his great hymn:

When peace like a river attendeth my way, when sorrows like sea billows roll;
Whatever my lot, Thou hast taught me to say, "It is well, it is well with my soul."[3]

(For the rest of the lyrics, you can look at your hymnal or search online.)

To be honest, I do not know if my faith is that strong. I know I struggled with God and begged Him to heal my daughter when she was hit by a car and the prognosis was grim. As I flew to France, where she was, God provided several people to pray with me. Then God ultimately healed my daughter, and He used that situation to allow me to witness to another woman.

My favorite part of studying Psalm 103 is seeing that the Lord does not treat us as we deserve. (Can you imagine what it would be like if He did?) Consider these things: The word *fear* means to respect or to hold in honor. The east and west will not ever meet. When God forgives sin, He removes it forever. God truly is a tender and loving Father who pours His love into us through the Holy Spirit. (See Romans 5:5.)

Questions for Thought

1. Think of a time in your life when things were rocky:

    a. Can you see how the Lord provided what was needed? Explain.

    b. What things in Psalm 103 will you remember to encourage yourself the next time the road gets rocky?

2. Stop and ask yourself and the Lord if your time with Him has become routine.

    a. If your time with God has become routine, how will you change that?

    b. Rewrite Psalm 103 in your own words, as if you were telling yourself and others about God.

3. Compare and contrast Moody and Spafford. What did they have in common? What did they lose? How did they deal with their losses?

CHAPTER 8

EYES SHUT, EARS OPEN

One of the hallmarks of MS is exhaustion. I do not mean just feeling tired. I mean a feeling of suddenly hitting a wall. It is a complete, sudden loss of energy. Heat can make the exhaustion worse. I try to plan around it. I balance my days, take naps, and take my medicine, but this affect is still frustrating.

Most people do not understand what I am experiencing. And I know I am guilty of putting on masks because I tire of people asking questions. Through it all, though, I am finding more and more that I must rely on the Lord for extra energy and guidance. The Lord is teaching me through this disease, and few of the lessons are easy. I am learning that I need to be more transparent. I am learning that I must ask for what I need and that I need to ask for help when I need it, instead of trying to do everything myself. I am learning that sometimes I can't do everything I would like to in one day; I have to take breaks and rest. I have to listen to my body. I have to write things down to remember them. Those are just some of the adjustments and "learning experiences" I am working on. Now, remember, I am a stubborn creature, a former R.N., who is accustomed to the role of caretaker. The Lord must continually remind me of the changes in my life. Yet, He also is able to use the changes.

Air exposure quickly takes freshness from food, but a little bit of lemon juice sprinkled on pieces of cut-up fruits or vegetables will help keep them fresh. After the items are cut, lemon juice will keep lettuce fresh, bananas yellow, celery from wilting, and apples from turning brown.

Much like fruits and vegetables lose their freshness when they're cut, we lose our energy and excitement for the Lord when we get exposed to the "air" of tribulations and stresses. Dealing with the daily grind of one day following another and keeping up with our husbands, children, jobs, homes, errands, commitments, and loneliness can all cause us to wilt, and everyone can see it. Or maybe we think it's necessary to put on one of those I'm-a-good-little-Christian masks; then we figure that no one can see our pain. *After all*, we think, *a "good Christian" doesn't have hard times.* We burrow into our holes, coming out only when we really must. We bathe in buckets of self-pity and if-onlys. We keep questioning our decisions, asking, "Why did you let me do that Lord?" and our worth, saying, "Why are you even keeping me around Lord?" We beat ourselves over the head while our Father watches and wishes we would simply listen to His Word. If we take the lemon juice of our struggles and turn it over to the Lord, trusting Him, He will keep us fresh and use that lemon juice to help us grow in Him.

Let me give you a bit of wisdom. Essentially, stuff happens. There is evil in this world. That's a fact. Our job is to keep our eyes on the One who defeated evil. He will guide us and comfort us. However, even though I know this, I forget it frequently. I seem to think I can do a much better job at handling my frustrations, even when I'm constantly getting into worse and worse trouble. If I'd just let my Father take care of me—keep me fresh—I wouldn't be in trouble. By trouble, I mean being focused in the wrong direction and on the wrong person. The lemon juice of my issues squirted me in the eyes, and now my eyes are burning and tearing. What I need to remember at times like these is that even if I can't see, I still can listen to the ever-present Lord. When I do that, then my mind remembers what my heart knows: I have nothing to fear.

Romans 8:15–17 says, "So you have not received a spirit that makes you fearful slaves. Instead, you received God's Spirit when he adopted you as his own children. Now we call him, 'Abba, Father.' For his Spirit joins with our spirit to affirm that we are God's children. And since we are his children, we are his heirs. In fact, together with Christ we are heirs of God's glory. But if we are to share his glory, we must also share his suffering" (NLT). Imagine that! You and I have the same Spirit that God has so that we can communicate with Him. We aren't pawns on a cosmic chessboard. Our spirits share the Spirit of God, and we can choose to go His way or ours.

Which way do you sense the Spirit telling you to go? It is a daily, sometimes hourly question because temptations and distractions beckon from everywhere. We need to work on constant communication with God.

Now think about this: we mere created human beings are directed to use the term "Daddy" when we call on the supreme Creator of the universe, who sent His Son for our redemption. "Abba" literally means "daddy." Some may have trouble with this, but I beg you to think about God as the Most Perfect Daddy, the one you dreamed about when you were little—the daddy who is always there for you, who loves to cuddle you, who stands up for you, and who never lets you down. I don't want to lower your thoughts about who God is, but I do want you to see the relationship He desires to have with you.

In addition to being children of the heavenly Father, we also are His heirs. That means Jesus, in a sense, is our Brother. Jesus didn't escape trials while He lived on earth, and He is God's Son. So if we are all in the same family, we must expect hard times. The difference is that we have each other and our Lord. By His life, He showed us how to endure, and the indwelling Holy Spirit, whom Jesus left here for us, helps us through the rough times.

Questions for Thought

1. What stage of life are you in?

2. Do you find yourself wearing a mask, even around your friends? Why?

3. What do you question about yourself?

4. What do you question about the Father and why?

5. What does it mean to you that we can call God "Abba" and are co-heirs with Christ?

6. Write down a description of the most perfect father you can imagine. That is your heavenly Father!

CHAPTER 9

WHERE DID THAT LEMON COME FROM?

I have always wondered if the notorious Tree of the Knowledge of Good and Evil was a lemon tree. Think about it. Lemons are pretty, yellow, and just begging to be handled and eaten … until that first bite. Then *wow*, the sour taste floods your mouth! Perhaps lemons did not start that way. As far as I know, the lemon is the only fruit that remains sour when it is ripe. Maybe the sour taste of the lemon is what it experienced as its consequence of the fall.

In order for a gardener to grow a lemon tree, a lemon has to be cut so that the seeds can be dug out. The seeds a gardener uses to grow trees must be the good ones, but cutting into the fruit to get those seeds does not sound pleasant, does it? It even sounds like surgery! In a sense, it is. And as it turns out, if the fruit is going to give of itself to allow another plant to exist, it must die.

You know, the Lord talked about planting seeds. In Matthew 13:31–32 (MSG) He says, "God's kingdom is like a pine nut that a farmer plants. It is quite small as seeds go, but in the course of years it grows into a huge pine tree, and eagles build nests in it." Matthew 13:3–8 (MSG) reads, "What do you make of this? A farmer planted seed. As he scattered the seed, some of it fell on the road, and birds ate it. Some fell in the gravel; it sprouted quickly but did not put down roots, so when the sun came up it withered just as quickly. Some fell in the weeds; as it came up, it was strangled by the weeds. Some fell on good earth, and produced a harvest beyond his wildest dreams." Then 2 Corinthians 9:6 (MSG) says, "Remember: A stingy planter gets a stingy crop; a lavish planter gets a lavish crop."

When the Lord wants to plant us someplace, He opens us up to remove the unproductive parts of our lives. He scoops into the lemon parts of us—the sour parts—and really digs to get rid of the nastiness. He knows us. We cannot hide anything from Him. Then He uses the productive parts for His glory. Funny thing, though, since we are not the Gardener, we do not get to decide which parts of our lives He will use.

After the farmer has seeds, the ground has to be cleared for planting. The weeds must be pulled, and a hole must be dug. In our lives, this is the part of the process when God allows and requires our participation. He picks the site of our service, but we must take part in being obedient. Sin chokes out the desire to allow the Lord to have His perfect way with our lives, so we must gamely pull on our gardening gloves and pull out the weeds of sin that will choke out the new growth that God is trying to cultivate. It might be tempting to look at the work involved and think, *Forget it!* But we must keep at it. We also need to remember that some weeds are deceptive. They look like flowers, but they are weeds all the same and need to be removed. Sins are like that too; they look innocent, but they are still sins and need to be pulled out of our lives.

Once the ground is prepared and the seeds are planted, watering is required. Despite its bad reputation, rain is essential in order for any plant to grow. It is the same for us. Even when we are planted exactly where God wants us to be, we can't expect the sun to shine all the time. Rain is necessary for proper, healthy growth.

Questions for Thought

1. What are the unproductive parts of your life that you will not let go?

2. What productive parts of your life are you hanging onto? (Sometimes things that are good are not God's best for you.)

3. Are there parts of your life that you are trying to hide from the Lord?

4. What sins in your life look innocent but can interfere with your relationship with the Lord?

5. When did Jesus say that we are not protected from bad things happening? What was His other promise connected with that?

6. Pray that the Lord searches your heart this week. Then open your heart to Him so that you can plant seeds with Him.

The best thing for us to do is surrender to God. Allow the Lord to search you. Allow the Lord to plant seeds with you. Not every plant will "come up," but the ones that the Lord wants to bear fruit will. Then accept the rain in your life. Christians cannot expect special treatment. Jesus said to expect hard times.

CHAPTER 10

LEMON DROPS

There seem to be times in our lives when we are pelted by lemons. Consider this: It takes about three years for a lemon tree to mature, and a new lemon tree is known to drop fruit. Why? The tree is still building its root structure and has to get rid of what it cannot handle, especially when it develops more fruit than it can support. The excess fruit needs to be dropped. This is normal and healthy.

Let's say for a minute that you are sitting under a lemon tree and lemons start dropping. What do you do? Yell at the tree? It's an inanimate object, so that really won't do any good. Do you stay under the tree? Do you ask God why this stupid tree is dropping lemons on you? Do you move?

I equate the sour times of life with being pelted by lemons. I recently went through a time when lemons were pelting me. Most of the lemons I could deal with, but the one that caused me to doubt the Lord was the one that also hit my daughter. When my daughter was overseas, she was hit by a car. The accident fractured her skull in two places. Immediately after the accident, she was not expected to live.

I flew to France to be with my daughter. During the entire flight, I alternated between praying and questioning God. *My daughter loves the Lord, why her? I have a chronic disease, why not let this happen to me?* However, all through the flight, the Lord surrounded me with Christians who somehow knew something was deeply wrong, and they prayed with me. All of them were strangers. No one could answer the "why" question, but the prayers calmed and refocused me.

When I made it to my daughter's side, I saw the CT scans, and yes, it was bad. All I could do was pray. I was helpless in every other area. I am a nurse, yes with MS, but I am still a nurse, and there I was, useless as my daughter lay in critical condition. Literally, all I could do was pray.

Then suddenly I realized that I had the wrong perspective. I could stay at her side and give her the best medicine: prayer. Also, I was able to send emails, and my church and many others prayed. By God's grace, today, my daughter is fine.

When lemons are pelting you, pray. Then move. You see, God can use even the sour lemon times for His purposes. While I was at the hospital with my daughter, I met a woman who had difficulties with depression and thoughts of suicide. Her English was poor, and my French was worse, but I found a way witness to her. I told her that she was God's princess, a daughter of the King. Now, I am not saying that my daughter had to be hit by a car for this woman to hear the gospel, but God can use lemons for His purposes.

How did God use my lemons for His purposes? God made me move. I, a very private person, shared my terror with strangers on a plane. All of the people I spoke with turned out to be Christians, and they prayed with me. The conversations deepened my faith and theirs and brought glory to God. Then I shared the gospel, witnessing of the reality and love of God even in tough situations (sadly, something I do not do very often) because I empathized with the woman at the hospital. The witness made a difference. It brought her closer to faith. Also, in addition to that woman's world being brightened, the neurologist working with my daughter was amazed by her recovery, and he became more open to faith. Through it all, my family's faith and the faith of those in my church was strengthened as a result of them being a part of this experience through their prayers.

Sometimes I yell at God in frustration because our family still has to deal with the aftermath of my daughter's accident—the physical therapy and the lingering effects of a severe head injury—but really, my daughter is fine. Thankfully, God can take my lashing out at Him because He understands my frustration and compassionately comforts me when my annoyance, impatience, and irritation begin to show. The tender truths from His Word calm me down and refocus my thoughts.

I cannot speak for God or assume the reason(s) why my daughter's accident happened, other than to say that we live in a world broken by sin. What I do know is that when my daughter was injured, God gave me the same choices He gives us all—whatever our circumstances are: follow Him or do not follow Him, trust Him or do not trust Him.

Bad things happen; yet that does not mean God is helpless or out of control. He used my daughter's accident to make my roots grow deeper in Him. He used it to make me grow healthy fruit. He did not do it by coercion; He did it through love. Everyone who heard of the accident was affected by it and had their eyes turned to God. They were witnesses to my daughter's stunning recovery. It is another reminder that God works all things for our good. Romans 8:28 (MSG) says, "That's why we can be so sure that every detail in our lives of love for God is worked into something good." And as Joseph said in Genesis 50:20 (MSG), "Don't you see, you planned evil against me but God used those same plans for my good, as you see all around you right now—life for many people."

Questions for Thought

1. Are you dealing with things that you cannot handle right now? What are they?

2. Picture your life as a tree. Where are your roots?

3. How deep are your roots? If a strong wind (difficult circumstance) came, would you blow over easily?

4. What do you do when "lemons" (several challenging circumstances) start falling on you?

5. Why isn't it healthy to sit and allow the "lemons" to pelt you?

6. Is it OK to yell at God? Why or why not?

7. How does being pelted with lemons sometimes cause you to grow in your Christian walk?

CHAPTER 11

THE COST OF BEAUTY

Lemons are enticing. Many lemon growers actually have to put nets over their trees to protect the fruit from birds. The bright color of the lemons draws the birds to the fruit. But they never eat all of a lemon; they just peck at it until it is useless to the grower. The birds never seem to learn that the beautifully colored fruit is sour. The growers try nets and hang shiny objects around the trees to frighten the birds, but still, a few hardy, stubborn, winged wonders persist at trying to get at the fruit.

I think that we are the same as those birds. Our eyes see something that seems to be just what we want, something that will fill our needs at the time. If we obtain it, much of the time, we do not even use all of it or take advantage of what the particular item offers. We just peck at it enough to explore it. We may even stick around long enough to discover that what we desired so very much is not what we really wanted at all, and then, the taste of it sours in our mouths.

The Lord tries to warn us. He puts "nets" over things we should not touch. However, stubborn creatures that we are, we ignore the warnings and plow ahead. We force our way through the netting of God's commandments to get to what we want, only to discover that the thing we were going after is sour. Why is that such a surprise?

Stubbornness is an attitude; in fact, the Hebrew root word for it stresses the attitude of the person. It describes a sulky attitude, much like a child acts when he or she is denied what he or she wants. It is a rebellious heart. This reminds me of 1 Kings 21:4 (MSG), which says, "Ahab went home in a black mood, sulking over Naboth the Jezreelite's words, 'I'll never turn over my family inheritance to you.' He went to bed, stuffed his face in his pillow, and refused to eat." What a pouting baby, and Ahab was the king! Psalms 78:8 (MSG) relates, "Heaven forbid they should be like their parents, bullheaded and bad, A fickle and faithless bunch who never stayed true to God."

Our attitudes trap us in the same way that nets trap birds. Let's face it; an attitude is a habit, and we can develop the habit of ignoring the warnings of God. When we ignore the Light and do what we wish, we come up with a mouthful of bitter juice. We are fortunate to have a God who can choose to gently warn His children, or strongly warn them, with consequences. Ezekiel 3:17 (BBE) says, "Son of man, I have made you a watchman for the children of Israel: so give ear to the word of my mouth, and give them word from me of their danger."

Psalms 19:9–11 (BBE) says, "The fear of the Lord is clean, and has no end; the decisions of the Lord are true and full of righteousness. More to be desired are they than gold, even than much shining gold; sweeter than the dropping honey. By them is your servant made conscious of danger, and in keeping them there is great reward."

It appears that while lemons are a necessary part of life, when God does not want us to go near the lemons, there is a price that we pay. We have a choice. Do we want to flirt with the sour taste and try to duck under the barriers that the Lord has placed, or do we want to use the issues that the sour things and times have put in our lives?

Do not think for a minute that the Lord does not care or is unaware of what is going on. He knows, He cares, and He is waiting with open arms for you to call out to Him. We may as well stay away from the lemons when God tells us to and taste the lemons and learn from the situation when we are pelted with them. Then perhaps the decisions we make the next time lemons come along will be better. We just need to remember that no matter what the situation, God loves us and He forgives us when we turn to Him in repentance. We need to run to Daddy—always.

Deuteronomy 30:19 (BBE) says, "Let heaven and earth be my witnesses against you this day that I have put before you life and death, a blessing and a curse: so take life for yourselves and for your seed." Joshua 24:15 (BBE) says, "And if it seems evil to you to be the servants of the Lord, make the decision this day whose servants you will be: of the gods whose servants your fathers were across the River, or of the gods of the Amorites in whose land you are living: but I and my house will be the servants of the Lord."

Questions for Thought

1. What attitudes do you have that get in the way of your relationship with God?

2. What do the above Scripture passages tell you about God?

3. Is there a decision that God is prompting you to make today? What is it?

4. How can you use the sour things that have slipped into your life?

CHAPTER 12

THE WORDS WE SPEAK

Did you know that you can gargle with lemon juice when you get a sore throat or have bad breath? Our throats can get sore from speaking too much, from common viruses, or from bacteria. And it seems that everyone has bad breath at one time or another. Much like our throats get sore or we get bad breath, we can speak sore or smelly words. Let's take some time to think about what comes out of our mouths. Consider these verses:

And the Lord said to Moses, "Say to all the people of Israel, You are to be holy, for I, the Lord your God, am holy."

—Leviticus 19:1–2 BBE

Let this book of the law be ever on your lips and in your thoughts day and night, so that you may keep with care everything in it; then a blessing will be on all your way, and you will do well.

—Joshua 1:8 BBE

In Old Testament times, the people only had the words of the prophets and the teachings of the priests. Today, we have a written Bible that is available in several translations, with a variety of features. We have study Bibles, Bibles for men, Bibles for women, Bibles for students, and Bibles for studious people. Yet, until 1445, the Old and New Testaments were not available for common people to read. However, most young Jewish men were thoroughly educated in their religion through the rabbis, via oral tradition.

Luke 6:43–45 (MSG) says, "You don't get wormy apples off a healthy tree, nor good apples off a diseased tree. The health of the apple tells the health of the tree. You must begin with your own life-giving lives. It's who you are, not what you say and do, that counts. Your true being brims over into true words and deeds." These verses are not just speaking of a tree and its fruit. It also applies to what flows out of our lives and mouths.

What comes from your mouth? I am not speaking of the times when people can hear you or of when fellow Christians can hear you. I am asking what comes from your mouth at other times, like when you are driving. What comes from your thoughts? How about those times when you didn't say what you were thinking but, if given the chance, you might have?

Matthew 15:8–11 (MSG) says, "'These people make a big show of saying the right thing, but their heart isn't in it. They act like they're worshiping me, but they don't mean it. They just use me as a cover for teaching whatever suits their fancy.' He then called the crowd together and said, 'Listen, and take this to heart. It's not what you swallow that pollutes your life, but what you vomit up.'" Mark 12:33 (MSG) says, "And loving him with all passion and intelligence and energy, and loving others as well as you love yourself. Why, that's better than all offerings and sacrifices put together!"

According to philosophers of the time, the conscience resided in the heart, which is why it is inherently wicked and needs God and His salvation. Biblically speaking, and to the Hebrews, the heart was and is the center of life and spirituality. The word *heart* actually was used by the Israelites and biblical writers as a synonym for the soul. The Hebrews cherished the Shema, which says, "Hear, oh Israel, the Lord is God, the Lord is One. Love the Lord your God with all your heart and with all your soul and with all your strength" (Deuteronomy 6:4–5). This was to be written on their hearts, souls, and minds. In fact, pious Jews would wear phylacteries on their foreheads, arms, and tucked into their garments. These were little boxes with pieces of Scripture in them, and they were worn to keep the Word of God ever close to the Israelites.

In Mark 12:29–31 (MSG), Jesus quoted the Shema: "The first in importance is, 'Listen, Israel: The Lord your God is one; so love the Lord God with all your passion and prayer and intelligence and energy.' And here is the second: 'Love others as well as you love yourself.' There is no other commandment that ranks with these."

Based on Scripture, it's reasonable to say that we need to watch our hearts. After all, Jesus said in Matthew 12:34, "For out of the overflow of the heart the mouth speaks." What starts out as a little seed of anger or bitterness or pride or covetousness not only dishonors the Giver of all things but also, if unobserved and unconfessed, grows and takes root, squeezing God out His rightful place in our hearts. And eventually, that anger, bitterness, guilt, or covetousness will come out of our mouths. In addition, not dealing with our feelings appropriately can make us physically sick. Ulcers, high blood pressure, and other illnesses can injure the body when we keep our emotions locked up.

Through the years, Scriptures have been twisted and turned to make any act "OK." And many people today believe they are only accountable to themselves. Scriptures are even sometimes thought of as old-fashioned fairy tales. Yet, all of the prophecies of the Messiah were fulfilled and time after time, God proves that what His Word says is true.

Questions for Thought

1. What does *holy* mean, and why is it so important to know its definition?

2. Why do we have to *know* the Bible?

3. Do a heart check right now. How is yours? What are your priorities? Do you have any bad seeds growing? Or is the Shema written on your heart?

4. What comes out of your mouth the most? Does it honor God?

PART THREE

THE "DEADLY SINS"

CHAPTER 13

LEMON JUICE REPELS ANTS

The hard times in life slow us down or may even shut us down. When hard times come in my life, I tend to wear masks. I do not often let people see the real me. I am afraid people will not like what they see and I will be hurt. I allow the past to control my present. However, life and new life in Christ cannot work that way. Masks leave too much room for bitterness and fear. Masks cause us to be afraid to move in any direction, and they render us unable to do anything for the Lord and can cause us to become lazy. What is being lazy? It is a lack of discipline in one's life. The Hebrew root word means a loose tongue or deceitful mind. The word refers to things that are trying, hefty, or stuck.[10] Jesus spoke of this in the parable of the three servants in Matthew 25.

Proverbs 6:6–8 (NLT) says, "Take a lesson from the ants, you lazybones. Learn from their ways and become wise! Though they have no prince or governor or ruler to make them work, they labor hard all summer, gathering food for the winter." These verses are talking about laziness. Laziness, being shut down and not doing anything, is one of the seven deadly sins. Why is laziness one of the seven deadly sins? Consider these additional verses:

The way of the lazy is overgrown with thorns, but the path of the upright is a level highway.
—Proverbs 15:19 NRSV

The appetite of the lazy craves, and gets nothing, while the appetite of the diligent is richly supplied.

—Proverbs 13:4 NRSV

Being lazy and thorny and not working for God or worshiping Him while expecting everything from the Lord or from some other source is sinful. Then we top it off by throwing a temper tantrum on an adult scale when we do not get what we want. We hide within a shield of thorny bushes, daring anyone to come near, even the Lord. I know because I have been in this very mindset. This is a deadly attitude to have because we are pushing away the One who can heal us.

Questions for Thought

1. When have you crawled into your patch of briars to hide?

2. Who brought you out? How?

3. What did you learn from that experience?

4. Is wearing a mask or "hiding," laziness? Why?

CHAPTER 14

LUST

Lust is defined as a passionate desire for something.[10] Unbelievably, lust (desire) can be a positive thing. Look at these verses:

> What the wicked dread will come upon them, but the desire of the righteous will be granted.
> —Proverbs 10:24 NRSV

> He said to them, I have eagerly desired to eat this Passover with you before I suffer.
> —Luke 22:15 NRSV

> I am hard pressed between the two: my desire is to depart and be with Christ, for that is far better. But to remain in the flesh is more necessary for you.
> —Philippians 1:23–24 NRSV

Obviously, none of these things is wrong. We all long to be with Christ, we all like to fellowship, and we all desire to be righteous. However, we can't become righteous on our own. We need Jesus for that. And as we walk with the Lord, we need our brothers and sisters in Christ to be there, encouraging and praying for us. We also need to wait for the Lord's timing and will. (For me, that is the hardest one.)

Lust can also be negative. We know that. I have lusted for many negative things. The corny saying, "Looking for love in all the wrong places," referred directly to me. But God wants us to put off the things of this world and desire Him. Ephesians 4:22–23 (NRSV) says, "You were taught to put away your former way of life, your old self, corrupt and deluded by its lusts, and to be renewed in the spirit of your minds." We must change our ways of thinking. We need to think about what we really want and focus on things that are eternal, not on what will crumble at the end of time. Colossians 3:5 (NRSV) says, "Put to death, therefore, whatever in you is earthly: fornication, impurity, passion [lust], evil desire, and greed (which is idolatry)."

Questions for Thought

1. Pray about this. What do you really want? For example, do you want people to notice you at church, or do you attend for a sincere worship experience?

2. Do you try to accomplish righteousness on your own? Are you thinking that when you get to heaven, you will be able to tell the Lord all your accomplishments to cover some of those besetting sins? What are some of those sins? Who really took care of them? Write a prayer about that.

3. Which is the hardest for you: waiting for the Lord's timing, waiting for the Lord's will, or simply walking with Him and seeing things as He does? Why?

4. Write a prayer about this also, asking the Lord to help you wait for His timing and to become more aware of His intervention.

CHAPTER 15

GLUTTONY

Stubbornness, rebellion, disobedience, drunkenness, and wastefulness are synonyms for *gluttony* in Hebrew. But *gluttony* translates even better in Hebrew as "good for nothing."[10] It's easy to see why gluttony is a sin. When we are overindulging or when what we want does not happen when we want it to happen, it's tempting to rebel against God, refuse to take part in His plans, and become absent from the community of believers. This weak point for me must have been a weak point for many because the Bible has a lot to say about gluttony. Here are some examples:

And say to them, This son of ours is hard-hearted and uncontrolled, he will not give attention to us; he gives himself up to pleasure and strong drink.

—Deuteronomy 21:20 BBE

Do not join those who drink too much wine or gorge themselves on meat, for drunkards and gluttons become poor, and drowsiness clothes them in rags.

—Proverbs 23:20–21

For you have spent enough time in the past doing what pagans choose to do—living in debauchery, lust, drunkenness, orgies, carousing and detestable idolatry.

—1 Peter 4:3

Through these Scriptures, and there are more, can you see how gluttony will take you down the wrong road quickly? Whatever is attracting you—food, money, status, entertainment, etc.—it literally makes you good for nothing. No one can be both a dedicated Christian and dedicated to the things of the world. As Luke 16:13 (WEY) says, "No servant can be in bondage to two masters. For either he will hate one and love the other, or else he will cling fast to one and scorn the other. You cannot be bondservants both of God and of gold."

As Christians, we have to make hard choices sometimes. We have to choose how we are going to spend our time and our money, and we must choose how to live out our values. The most important choice we have to make is *who* is most important to us. Making choices in these areas is not always easy, but everyone must face such decisions.

Questions for Thought

1. Do you have a tendency to be stubborn? (Come on now; be honest.) Confess it to the Lord. Write your prayer here:

2. Why is gluttony a major sin?

3. Who is most important to you? Is it really Christ? Is this question something you need to pray about? Start your prayer here, and keep a journal, chronicling how you deal with this question over time.

CHAPTER 16

ENVY

Envy is a resentful or painful awareness of someone's advantage and the desire to have the same thing.[10] Covetousness is a bit different. Coveting leads to desire and then seeks to violate the rights of others by taking for oneself what others have.[10] These may be material things or status.

I know that I do envy others for their material blessings and their health. I also envy other people's marriages. But I have to keep in mind that God gave me what I have, and I must learn to be content with it.

Envy was the motive for arresting Jesus. Did you know that? As Matthew tells the story of Christ's arrest, trials, and crucifixion, he is mentioning Pilate. As the disciple explains, "For he knew it was out of envy that they had handed Jesus over to him" (Matthew 27:18).

Envy comes out of a person and defiles him or her. In his gospel, Mark explains, "What comes out of a man is what makes him unclean. For from within, out of men's hearts, come evil thoughts, sexual immorality, theft, murder, adultery, greed, malice, deceit, lewdness, envy, slander, arrogance and folly. All these evils come from inside and make a man unclean" (Mark 7:20–23).

Envy is also a characteristic of opposing the gospel. Acts 5:16–18 states, "Crowds gathered also from the towns around Jerusalem, bringing their sick and those tormented by evil spirits, and all of them were healed. Then the high priest and all his associates, who were members of the party of the Sadducees, were filled with jealousy. They arrested the apostles and put them in the public jail."

Even as bad as envy is, God's response to such sinful longings of the human heart is to give us more grace. Isn't that just like our Father?

Questions for Thought

1. What do you think the difference is between envy and covetousness? (I personally stick to dictionary definitions, even though some make the two words sound the same.)

2. What are the longings of your heart?

3. What things do you need to talk to your Father about? Write them down, and put into action whatever you know you ought to do. First John 1:9 promises, "If we confess our sins, he is faithful and just and will forgive us our sins and purify us from all unrighteousness."

CHAPTER 17

COVETOUSNESS

Covetousness is another deadly sin. It is the desire to have what belongs to others, and it leads to the downfall of many powerful people.[10] Look at these verses:

Greed causes fighting; trusting the Lord leads to prosperity.

—Proverbs 28:25 NLT

You can be sure that no immoral, impure, or greedy person will inherit the Kingdom of Christ and of God. For a greedy person is an idolater, worshiping the things of this world.

—Ephesians 5:5 NLT

Colossians 3:5 says that greed is idolatry. So it is safe to say that coveting is worshiping anything other than God. That is why it is deadly. It is insidious. A person can worship something as simple as sports above God, choosing to stay home to watch a game instead of going to worship and valuing his or her "down time" more than time with God. A person can worship his or her job above God by putting it before Him or by ignoring actions that are against His precepts but excusing them, saying, "It's just business." This person values money or climbing higher in the company over God. A person also can worship social approval, the latest fashions, the latest computer, or even his or her own children, putting them before God.

I think you get the idea. We tend to give God our leftovers, whether it is our time or our money. I've even heard people make excuses for giving God leftovers. They say things like, "Oh, but God will understand!" Well, no, throughout the Bible, God says that He is the only God and we are to put *nothing* and no one before Him. Deuteronomy 5:7–10 states, "You shall have no other gods before [aside from] me. You shall not make for yourself an idol in the form of anything in heaven above or on the earth beneath or in the waters below. You shall not bow down to them or worship them; for I, the Lord your God, am a jealous God, punishing the children for the sin of the fathers to the third and fourth generation of those who hate me, but showing love to a thousand generations of those who love me and keep my commandments."

All excuses for putting God second fly out the window. Every time that you and I put Him second or third in our lives, it is sin. Everything that we have comes from Him (I think we all tend to forget that).

Sometimes, we have a temptation to do "good" things for the wrong reasons. In other words, we do things just to make sure that we are noticed for being such "great" Christians. Consider what Jesus says in John 8:54–59:

> "If I glorify myself, my glory means nothing. My Father, whom you claim as your God, is the one who glorifies me. Though you do not know him, I know him. If I said I did not, I would be a liar like you, but I do know him and keep his word. Your father Abraham rejoiced at the thought of seeing my day; he saw it and was glad."
>
> "You are not yet fifty years old," the Jews said to him, "and you have seen Abraham!"
>
> "I tell you the truth," Jesus answered, "before Abraham was born, I am!" At this, they picked up stones to stone him, but Jesus hid himself, slipping away from the temple grounds.

Even Jesus did not seek attention for Himself. Jesus wanted all glory to go to His Father. I AM is the name God told Moses to call Him in Exodus 3:14: "I AM WHO I AM. This is what you are to say to the Israelites: 'I AM has sent me to you.'" The longer form of the name is more a description of who God is rather than a simple name. It describes what God does, that He is without limits, and that He may act as He wishes. Consider the following verses.

> For in bringing many sons to glory, it was entirely appropriate that God—all things exist for Him and through Him—should make the source of their salvation perfect through sufferings. For the One who sanctifies and those who are sanctified all have one Father. That is why Jesus is not ashamed to call them brothers.
>
> —Hebrews 2:10–11 HCSB

> But the Lord is the true God; he is the living God, the eternal King. When he is angry, the earth trembles; the nations cannot endure his wrath. "Tell them this: 'These gods, who did not make the heavens and the earth, will perish from the earth and from under the heavens.'"
>
> —Jeremiah 10:10–11

See now that I myself am He! There is no god besides me. I put to death and I bring to life, I have wounded and I will heal, and no one can deliver out of my hand.

—Deuteronomy 32:39

Come, let us bow down in worship, let us kneel before the Lord our Maker; for he is our God and we are the people of his pasture, the flock under his care.

—Psalms 95:6–7

As far as wanting more than we have, we must remember that God is the One who provides everything. Are you ready to tell Him that what He's given you is not enough? That is what jealousy is. We compare ourselves to others. We need to learn to be thankful and content and let God be God.

Questions for Thought

1. When do you feel jealous and slip into covetousness?

2. Take an honest look at your schedule. Do you have daily time with God? Do you participate in weekly fellowship by attending church services? If you don't have time alone with God, when will you start? If you don't go to church, when will you start? If you do have daily devotions and attend church, how can you make these times more meaningful?

3. How do you participate in the deadly sin of covetousness, and how will you deal with it?

4. What things may you be doing that are "right" for the wrong reasons?

5. Read over the scriptures in this chapter, think about the questions, and write a prayer to God in your journal. Remember, prayer is simply a conversation with God.

CHAPTER 18

PRIDE

Why am I writing this book? Why am I allowing strangers to take a glimpse into my life? It's simple: I am doing this for the Lord. I have nothing to be proud of; I cannot hide my sins from the Lord. I want others to learn that the hard times of life, the sour times, are not punishment. Also, we should not take pride in getting through the rough patches of life. Instead, we should use the lessons we learn from these hard times to help others.

Some grocery stores apply lemon wax to produce to make it shinier. In many ways, we are like those grocers; we want to present ourselves as being "shinier" for the Lord. However, we really have nothing to be proud of. He was the One who bore the burden of our sins. He gave us our spiritual gifts. It is our job to use those gifts to glorify Him and to share His love with others.

Zadon is the Hebrew noun that translates as "pride," "insolence," "presumptuousness," or "arrogance." The noun is formed from the verbal root *zud* or *zid*, meaning "to boil up, to act proudly, presumptuously, or rebelliously." Two adjectives from this same root, *zed* and *zedon*, mean "insolent," "presumptuous," or "raging." (See the *Holman Treasury of Key Bible Words*.) These words usually referred to when people were acting proudly against the priests, the judge, or worse, the Lord. Judgment for *zadon* (pride) was immediate death.[10]

However, there is nothing wrong with boasting in the Lord. Second Corinthians 10:17 states, "Let him who boasts boast in the Lord." Jeremiah 9:24 says, "'But let him who boasts boast about this: that he understands and knows me, that I am the Lord, who exercises kindness, justice and righteousness on earth, for in these I delight,' declares the Lord."

Consider some other verses related to pride:

Haughty eyes and a proud heart, the lamp of the wicked, are sin!

—Proverbs 21:4

He mocks proud mockers but gives grace to the humble.

—Proverbs 3:34

Come unto me, all ye labouring and burdened ones, and I will give you rest, take up my yoke upon you, and learn from me, because I am meek and humble in heart, and ye shall find rest to your souls, for my yoke is easy, and my burden is light.

—Matthew 11:28–30 YLT

Let me repeat that. We have nothing to be proud of; we all sin. Otherwise, we wouldn't need Jesus. He scoffs at the proud; He sees right through them. He knows what they are doing, thinking, and intending. Proud mockers are those who walk away from God's promises, those who jeer at Him—maybe even those who have been a little afraid to stand up for their faith.

Refusing to allow others to help us is also a form of pride. (That hurts!) I am self-sufficient, or I was until the MS effected me. I still fall into traps of wanting to do everything myself when I can't. I am not permitting others to use their gifts of mercy and hospitality when I do this. I am once again hiding behind my "wall."

As Christians, we must not do any of these things; if we do, we lose our humility, our grace, and the chance to be kind. The Lord's yoke simply joins us all together with Him. Jesus carries the maximum weight, *if* we allow Him to do so, and we become the body of Christ that He intended when we are using our various gifts to build each other up. Then we are building up the church instead of drawing all the attention to ourselves. The glory belongs to God and His Son, Christ Jesus.

Questions for Thought

1. Examine yourself. Don't let the plank in your own eye blind you. (See Matthew 7:3–5.)

2. Stop working so hard to be the perfect Christian. Yes, you read that right. No, I don't mean to go out carousing, but relax in your Shepherd's arms. What does He require from you? (See Micah 6:8 and Ecclesiastes 12:13.)

3. Are you still zealous for the Lord? Why or why not?

CHAPTER 19

ANGER

Anger is the last of our seven deadly sins. The anger being spoken of here isn't just a mild upset; it's a poisonous rage, a violent passion.[10] Consider these scriptures concerning anger:

Bridle your anger, trash your wrath, cool your pipes—it only makes things worse.

—Psalms 37:8 MSG

Post this at all the intersections, dear friends: Lead with your ears, follow up with your tongue, and let anger straggle along in the rear. God's righteousness doesn't grow from human anger. So throw all spoiled virtue and cancerous evil in the garbage. In simple humility, let our gardener, God, landscape you with the Word, making a salvation-garden of your life.

—James 1:19–21 MSG

If anyone boasts, "I love God," and goes right on hating his brother or sister, thinking nothing of it, he is a liar. If he won't love the person he can see, how can he love the God he can't see? The command we have from Christ is blunt: Loving God includes loving people. You have to love both.

—1 John 4:20–21 MSG

Wow! Those verses leave a sour enough taste in our mouths to make us pucker when people push our anger buttons. After reading those passages, we probably automatically think questions like:

1. What about the constant verbal abuse I've lived with?
2. What about those terrible things that person over there has done?
3. What about that terrible driver?

Can you still justify your anger against these people? Are you holding grudges?

All I can say is that Scripture is always right. I really don't have anything to be angry about. Think about it. God *had* to send His own Son to save His created beings just because they couldn't follow a few simple directions. Who do you think has more of a right to be angry—His created beings or God? Let's face it: we can't love God without loving people. People are created in His image.

Proverbs 25:28 says, "A person without self-control is like a house with its doors and windows knocked out" (MSG). This type of anger shows that self is still firmly planted on the throne. Thankfully, God handles His anger much differently than we do. Psalms 103:8–9 says, "The Lord is compassionate and gracious, slow to anger, abounding in love. He will not always accuse, nor will he harbor his anger forever." And Psalms 11:4 declares, "The Lord is in his holy temple; the Lord is on his heavenly throne."

We have to let God lead and "landscape" us and prune us. That is why I included the "seven deadly sins" in this section. As we grow in Christ, He will prune and shape us so that we become more like Him.

Questions for Thought

1. Who should be on the throne of your life? Why?

2. Why can't we love God without loving people?

3. Search your heart for the kind of anger that resides in it. Talk to the Lord, journal, and pray about your anger, remembering that God is the perfect Father.

PART FOUR

THE FRUIT

CHAPTER 20

PEACE

Peace is usually translated as quietness or rest.[10] Peace or rest is important to me. I have to manage stress and get more than enough rest because I have MS—too much stress brings a worsening of symptoms. I am required to trust God, especially during trials. If I do not, I hurt my relationship with Him and hurt myself. Ironically, it took having a serious illness for me to realize the importance of trusting God.

Psalm 37:7 (NRSV) clearly says, "Be still before the Lord and wait patiently for him; fret not yourself over the one who prospers in his way, over the man who carries out evil devices!" God calls us to be at peace even in the middle of trials. His peace never ends, nor does it have small print or "catches." Look at what the Bible has to say about peace:

Peace I leave with you; my peace I give to you. I do not give to you as the world gives. Do not let your hearts be troubled, and do not let them be afraid.

—John 14:27 NRSV

I have said this to you, so that in me you may have peace. In the world you face persecution. But take courage; I have conquered the world!

—John 16:33 NRSV

For he is our peace; in his flesh he has made both groups into one and has broken down the dividing wall, that is, the hostility between us.

—Ephesians 2:14 NRSV

For in him all the fullness of God was pleased to dwell, and through him God was pleased to reconcile to himself all things, whether on earth or in heaven, by making peace through the blood of his cross.

—Colossians 1:19–20 NRSV

Peace can also be a verb. In the original language, it means to make amends, to repay, and to make restitution.[10] This is why Christ is our peace. When He died, the veil that divided the Holy of Holies from the Holy place was torn from top to bottom. The High Priest was the only person permitted to enter the Holy of Holies and only once a year, on the Day of Atonement. The veil was too thick and too tall to be torn by human hands. Only One could have torn it from top to bottom. Now we can go before God's "throne of grace with confidence, so that we may receive mercy and find grace to help us in our time of need" (Hebrews 4:16).

Questions for Thought

1. Why was the veil torn? *It was to show that there is no longer a wall between us and God. We can talk to him face to face*

2. Why is Christ our peace?

3. Why must we be still and wait for the Lord in our circumstances? *God said "Be still and wait on the Lord"*

4. Write a prayer, telling God about an area in which you need peace.

CHAPTER 21

PATIENCE

I will freely tell you that I need a lot of help with patience. I used to joke that I used it all up at work and had nothing left for home. But I wasn't really joking.

Patience means an *active* endurance of opposition.[10] It is not passive. God is patient (thank heavens). Romans 2:3–4 says, "Do you imagine, whoever you are, that when you judge those who do such things and yet do them yourself, you will escape the judgment of God? Or do you despise the riches of his kindness and forbearance and patience? Do you not realize that God's kindness is meant to lead you to repentance?" (NRSV). James 5:10 says, "As an example of suffering and patience, beloved, take the prophets who spoke in the name of the Lord.

Patience is something a believer must grow into; the Spirit does not just fly by and dump a bunch of patience on a person. Patience is a key factor in spiritual growth" (NRSV). And Luke 8:15, from the parable of the sower, states, "But as for that in the good soil, these are the ones who, when they hear the word, hold it fast in an honest and good heart, and bear fruit with patient endurance" (NRSV).

Patience is not lying down and being a doormat. We are to remember God's patience with us and, by His grace and strength, extend patience to others.

Questions for Thought

1. Were you under the impression that to keep the peace, you had to be a doormat? Why? Ask the Lord for a better idea.

2. God's kindness is meant to lead people into repentance. What do you need to repent of?

3. Look up stories about some of the prophets. What kinds of things did they suffer?

4. What Scripture verse(s) do you "hold fast" to when you feel anger brewing?

CHAPTER 22

KINDNESS

Kindness is translated as either compassion or faithfulness to a person's relatives and friends. Kindness is a characteristic of true love. It can also be seen as moral excellence and mercy.[10] However, kindness is not an easy virtue. I have been hurt, but I am commanded to treat those responsible for that hurt with kindness. I am also commanded to forgive and, the hardest thing, not to carry a grudge. I am to treat every person as if he or she were Jesus and the way Jesus treats me. Ephesians 2:1–10 (NRSV) says:

> You were dead through the trespasses and sins in which you once lived, following the course of this world, following the ruler of the power of the air, the spirit that is now at work among those who are disobedient. All of us once lived among them in the passions of our flesh, following the desires of flesh and senses, and we were by nature children of wrath, like everyone else. But God, who is rich in mercy, out of the great love with which he loved us even when we were dead through our trespasses, made us alive together with Christ —by grace you have been saved—and raised us up with him and seated us with him in the heavenly places in Christ Jesus, so that in the ages to come he might show the immeasurable riches of his grace in kindness toward us in Christ Jesus. For by grace you have been saved through faith, and this is not your own doing; it is the gift of God—not the result of works, so that no one may boast. For we are what he has made us, created in Christ Jesus for good works, which God prepared beforehand to be our way of life.

Romans 11:22 says, "Note then the kindness and the severity of God: severity toward those who have fallen, but God's kindness toward you, provided you continue in his kindness; otherwise you also will be cut off" (NRSV).

The first thing to keep in mind is that none of us can claim moral excellence. Not one of us is a saint. We all have our little foibles. We were doomed because of our sin, and it is only through Christ's work that we are saved. Moreover, we are raised up and seated with Him. It's like going to a banquet with the President—but better. We are seated with Christ. I do not deserve that, but by His grace, I'm there. God is kind. We should be in the alley, begging scraps from the table, but we are not, so we need to share His kindness.

Questions for Thought

1. What do you think about when you contemplate being seated with Jesus?

2. How are you showing others the riches of God's grace to you?

3. Once again, our sins confront us. First John 1:9–10 reads, "If we confess our sins, he who is faithful and just will forgive us our sins and cleanse us from all unrighteousness. If we say that we have not sinned, we make him a liar, and his word is not in us" (NRSV).

4. Praise, confession, and requests: write some down now. The Lord is so very kind. Make it a daily habit to call to mind what God has done.

CHAPTER 23

GOODNESS

Here, goodness is an element of the fruit referring to those exhibiting a principled condition of the heart, those who try to live their lives within the boundaries of God's will.[10] Ephesians 5:8–11 says, "For you were once darkness, but now you are light in the Lord. Live as children of light (for the fruit of the light consists in all goodness, righteousness and truth), and find out what pleases the Lord. Have nothing to do with the fruitless deeds of darkness, but rather expose them."

What are some other things the Bible has to say about goodness?

Dear friend, do not imitate what is evil but what is good. Anyone who does what is good is from God. Anyone who does what is evil has not seen God.

—3 John 1:11

And do not think you can say to yourselves, "We have Abraham as our father." I tell you that out of these stones God can raise up children for Abraham. The ax is already at the root of the trees, and every tree that does not produce good fruit will be cut down and thrown into the fire.

—Matthew 3:9–10

The religious people, the synagogue leaders of Jesus' day, thought that they had the "in" with God. They could judge, exclude, and murder whoever they pleased. They even formed a coalition with the occupying Roman government so that they could continue to do their "thing" in peace. The Roman representative didn't want trouble, and those religious leaders knew that. The unspoken deal was *if the Jews were "good," the Romans would be relatively "good."* Therefore, the religious leaders put up with having to change the Roman coins, which had a graven image on them, into an acceptable coin for a small fee. Yet, no one accepted the moneychangers or the tax collectors, even though it was Herod who ordered them to raise most of the taxes so that he could build the temple.

Corruption was everywhere, from the priests all the way to Herod, and even to Caesar. The problem for all these higher-ups was that Jesus had this "terrible" habit of exposing corruption. He was honest. He was *not* a politician. He said what He meant and meant what He said. This is part of what led to His death. He told everyone what those leaders really were like without mincing words. He knew Scripture better than anyone else knew it. The people loved Him. Yet, until Peter's confession of faith, no one saw Him for who He really was. In Matthew 16:13–16 (MSG) it says, "When Jesus arrived in the villages of Caesarea Philippi, he asked his disciples, 'What are people saying about who the Son of Man is?' They replied, 'Some think he is John the Baptizer, some say Elijah, some Jeremiah or one of the other prophets.' He pressed them, 'And how about you? Who do you say I am?' Simon Peter said, 'You're the Christ, the Messiah, the Son of the living God.'" Think for a moment about how Jesus must have felt prior to Peter's confession. After all the signs, teaching, and knowledge from a man who was raised in a hamlet, they still did not get it.

What would Jesus say about us? We go to church, Sunday school, and Bible studies, but do we apply what we learn? That was the problem with the Jews of Jesus' era; they knew the Law, they kept most of the Law, but they did not know or love the Lawgiver.

Questions for Thought

1. How do you sometimes allow a person's behavior to blind you to his or her true character?

2. How can you change your preconceived ideas about others?

3. What kinds of people think they have an "in" with God? Do they really?

4. How do *you* blind yourself to who Jesus is?

CHAPTER 24

FAITHFULNESS

Faithful can mean devoted to duty or fidelity.[10] Read these verses about faithfulness:

Whoever can be trusted with very little can also be trusted with much, and whoever is dishonest with very little will also be dishonest with much.

—Luke 16:10

I thank Christ Jesus our Lord, who has given me strength, that he considered me faithful, appointing me to his service.

—1 Timothy 1:12

In addition to all this, take up the shield of faith, with which you can extinguish all the flaming arrows of the evil one.

—Ephesians 6:16

Faith is essential to our walk. Our faith can protect us from those thoughts and "lemons" being thrown at us. I don't mean we should walk around, grudgingly muttering to ourselves, "I believe, I believe, I believe." I mean we should possess a faith that lives through all circumstances. If we ask for faith to deal with the circumstances, Christ will help us. He is always faithful.

Do you remember Job? Job was a man who loved God and worshiped Him faithfully. Satan was "slightly" irked by this and approached God, claiming that Job's faithfulness existed only because life was going so well for him. In light of this accusation, God gave Satan permission to do anything he wanted to Job's blessings, as long as he did not hurt Job physically. Job lost everything: his fortune, his children, and his home; yet, he still praised God.

This irked Satan even more. Satan went back to God, demanding that He strike Job physically. Instead, God gave Satan permission to afflict Job, but He withheld permission to kill Job. After the devil severely distressed Job and ruined his health, Job's wife (who had been spared) told Job to "curse God and die." But he said to her, "'You speak as one of the foolish women speaks. Shall we indeed accept good from God, and shall we not accept adversity?' In all this Job did not sin with his lips" Job 2:10 (NKJV). Job did, however, curse the day he was born.

The first friend who arrived to mourn Job's losses with him and give him advice told him he must have brought everything on himself. Therefore, Job asked God what he did. There was no answer.

Job's second friend told Job that God does not reject a blameless man. The third friend said that everything would be all right.

The judgment in his friends' advice hit Job like they were beating a wounded puppy. These three friends and another friend berated Job (chapter after chapter) until Job broke down. It was then that God answered Job, in front of his friends, out of a storm. Job 38:3–21 (MSG) says (by the way, I really like this translation):

Pull yourself together, Job! Up on your feet! Stand tall! I have some questions for you, and I want some straight answers. Where were you when I created the earth? Tell me, since you know so much! Who decided on its size? Certainly, you'll know that! Who came up with the blueprints and measurements? How was its foundation poured, and who set the cornerstone, While the morning stars sang in chorus and all the angels shouted praise? And who took charge of the ocean when it gushed forth like a baby from the womb? That was me! I wrapped it in soft clouds, and tucked it in safely at night. Then I made a playpen for it, a strong playpen so it couldn't run loose, And said, "Stay here, this is your place. Your wild tantrums are confined to this place." And have you ever ordered Morning, "Get up!" told Dawn, "Get to work!" So you could seize Earth like a blanket and shake out the wicked like cockroaches? As the sun brings everything to light, brings out all the colors and shapes, The cover of darkness is snatched from the wicked—they're caught in the very act! Have you ever gotten to the true bottom of things, explored the labyrinthine caves of deep ocean? Do you know the first thing about death? Do you have one clue regarding death's dark mysteries? And do you have any idea how large this earth is? Speak up if you have even the beginning of an answer. Do you know where Light comes from and where Darkness lives So you can take them by the hand and lead them home when they get lost? Why, of course you know that.

I don't see God's answering Job as a Father chastising His child. I see it as God affirming the fact that He is in control. I see this as a reality check. God is the Creator, the Life-giver. He is faithful, and we must be careful to whom we listen. What were Job's "friends" doing? They were trying to place the blame for Job's misfortune on Job. They reasoned that he must have sinned terribly to make God punish him that way. His "friends" had no idea, well, neither did Job, about what was really going on. Yet Job stayed faithful. Yes, he questioned God, but he did not lose his faith.

After all was said and done, the Lord restored what Satan stole from Job because Job was faithful to God. Yes, Job got angry and let his emotions loose, but he never gave up on his faith, as much as his friends wanted him to. I know I said that twice; I want you to remember it.

When things happen all at once, or at the wrong time, it is normal to question God. I miscarried after begging and pleading for a child. I felt furious with God. I went through the same thing as Job. Several other things happened around the same time. Then later on, when my daughter was only nine months old, I slipped two discs, and then my son was diagnosed with ADHD. The only choice available to me, if I planned to get through that phase of my life, was to trust God.

Questions for Thought

1. Psalms 9:10 says, "Those who know your name will trust in you, for you, Lord, have never forsaken those who seek you." Knowing God's name means knowing God's character. (It may be helpful for you to go through and study all of God's names—when you are done with this study, of course!)Which aspect of God's character helps you to trust Him? Why?

2. Have you had "helpful friends" like Job? What's the best way to deal with them?

3. Is it OK to get angry with God? Why or why not?

CHAPTER 25

GENTLENESS

Consider the following scriptures regarding gentleness:

You have also given me the shield of Your salvation; your right hand has held me up, your gentleness has made me great.

—Psalm 18:35 NKJV

Take my yoke upon you and learn from me, for I am gentle and humble in heart, and you will find rest for your souls.

—Matthew 11:29

But the wisdom that is from above is first pure, then peaceable, gentle, willing to yield, full of mercy and good fruits, without partiality and without hypocrisy. Now the fruit of righteousness is sown in peace by those who make peace.

—James 3:17–18 NKJV

This is the gentleness of Christ, who approached the shunned, like the tax collectors, the woman with the issue of blood, and the woman caught in the act of adultery. (Where was the man?) Jesus is patient, mild—but it is a royal mildness—and humble. This is the Christ who dignified women. He loves all, even me. That is what drew me to Him.

Matthew 19:13–15 says, "One day some parents brought their children to Jesus so he could lay his hands on them and pray for them. However, the disciples scolded the parents for bothering him. But Jesus said, 'Let the children come to me. Don't stop them! For the Kingdom of Heaven belongs to those who are like these children.' And he placed his hands on their heads and blessed them before he left" (NLT). Jesus was always dignified, but His heart always showed through too. Children loved Him, and He loved them.

God refers to us as His children. He treats us with the same gentleness that Jesus showed the children. We are expected to do the same with others. There is no room in our Christian family for gossiping or hurting each other. But there is a responsibility to help each other the best we can during rough times.

Christ loved the outcasts of society. He horrified the religious leaders because the outcasts were ceremonially unclean. Christ cured lepers, healed women, forgave women, and the list goes on. Yet, He always had the Jewish people that He healed go to the temple to offer the appropriate sacrifices. Christ also loved children. Every time the disciples tried to drive them away, He gathered them. His spirit could not contain His love.

Questions for Thought

1. Gentleness is a spiritual gift. When we use it, we are showing others an imitation of Christ (Galatians 5:22). How has He treated you with gentleness? How have you treated others with gentleness?

2. Because gentleness is a spiritual gift, what can you do today to begin growing in it?

3. Do your children know about Jesus? Have you started to teach them? How can you start making Him more real to them? Write your action plan down.

CHAPTER 26

SELF-CONTROL

Self-control is usually translated as temperance, having continence, and holding in one's passions or desires.[10] Self-control is a virtue that I need help with in many aspects of my life. For example, I like to write, but only when I feel like writing. In other words, I do not like deadlines. In contrast, I can be too self-controlled when we talk about feelings. Yes, self-control is a spiritual gift, according to Galatians 5:23, but that is not an excuse for not exercising *some* self-control. A person cannot say, "Well, that is just not my gift," and then blow up.

Second Peter 1:5–8 says, "For this very reason, make every effort to add to your faith goodness; and to goodness, knowledge; and to knowledge, self-control; and to self-control, perseverance; and to perseverance, godliness; and to godliness, brotherly kindness; and to brotherly kindness, love. For if you possess these qualities in increasing measure, they will keep you from being ineffective and unproductive in your knowledge of our Lord Jesus Christ." Romans 13:14 states, "Rather, clothe yourselves with the Lord Jesus Christ, and do not think about how to gratify the desires of the sinful nature."

In the verses above, do you see the progression we need to go through in order to gain self-control? It is *not* usually something we can do on our own. Christians don't "just accept Christ" and quit there. Being a Christian is a *growing* process. We begin by accepting the Lord, and He gives us the Holy Spirit. Next, we learn more about God through Bible study, fellowship, and church attendance. We also learn to control our inner desires for the benefit of others, Christ, and ourselves. When we are discouraged and our faith is mocked, we learn to endure faithfully during times of attack. Christ was mocked, and we aren't better than He is. Each day that we walk with the Lord, we continue to grow in Him.

We are instructed to be kind and loving because these qualities make us more like Christ and show His character to the world. It's not a question of choosing who we want to exhibit these behaviors toward; it's a question of who we are and who God wants us to be. Self-controlled, Christ-like people who are spirit-filled draw others to Him.

Questions for Thought

1. Of the gifts listed in the verses from Peter, in which one(s) do you think you need a "boost"?

2. How do you feel about your effectiveness and productivity for God, as well as your knowledge of Jesus? How do you plan to improve these things?

3. Remember, a beautiful, new outfit—the character of the Holy Spirit—has been purchased for us. How are you going to *choose* to grow into it so you can wear it well?

PART FIVE

HOW MANY LEMONS IS IT GOING TO TAKE?

CHAPTER 27

HOW MANY LEMONS DOES IT TAKE?

One pound of lemons is equal to approximately four to five medium, whole lemons and 2/3 to 1 cup of juice. One medium lemon equals approximately 2 to 3 tablespoons of juice, 2 teaspoons of grated peel, and seven to ten slices.

In my life, there definitely have been times when I felt like I was being pelted with lemons. However, I realize now that maybe Satan's not the only one throwing them. The Lord may be trying to get my attention with those lemons. The Lord can permit adverse circumstances to come into a person's life to get his or her attention, and He has gotten my attention that way before.

Bad things happen for three reasons: First, we live in a fallen world. Second, Satan is prowling around, looking to destroy. Third, we make boneheaded decisions that bring negative circumstances upon ourselves. God allows bad things to touch us, but we get to choose whether or not we will take those things and use them for God's glory and to grow in Him.

As I said, Satan is prowling around, looking to destroy, so sometimes bad things happen because he is attacking. That may seem fanciful to some, but he is real, and he does like to mess with those who God loves. The simplest way for him to attack is to find a "foothold" or a way to control our responses.

I don't get angry easily, but some topics or issues will trigger a surprising result. I can be angry, but like any other Christian, I do not have permission to sin. Ephesians 4:26 (NLT) says, "Don't sin by letting anger control you." In contrast to my response when I am angry, my response when I am hurt is to withdraw, kind of like a turtle. This keeps me from ministering to those who need me.

Do you see? There is nothing wrong with feeling angry, unless that anger controls you or hurts someone. There also is nothing wrong with feeling hurt, unless it controls you to the point that it keeps you from ministry. People have emotions just like Jesus has emotions. It is how we use these emotions that can get us into one of Satan's snares.

We have a Lord who knows us and knows what life is like. He is not aloof. He is *with* us. The closeness we as Christians experience with our God is unique, especially when compared to all other belief systems.

First Peter 2:21 reads, "For to this you have been called, because Christ also suffered for you, leaving you an example, so that you should follow in his steps" (NRSV). How we handle the circumstances in our lives exhibits to others that we follow God. He gives us strength, and that witness attracts others to Him.

Hebrews 2:18 says, "Because he himself was tested by what he suffered, he is able to help those who are being tested" (NRSV). We have a God who knows everything that we go through: all the hurts, all the pain, all the suffering. He is not so high and lofty that He is immune or untouchable to us. On the contrary, He became one of us, and He knows how to help us.

Romans 8:35 states, "Who will separate us from the love of Christ? Will hardship, or distress, or persecution, or famine, or nakedness, or peril, or sword?" (NRSV). The early Christians died hideous deaths. Some even died before roaring crowds in the Roman coliseum as entertainment for the sick and twisted ungodly. Yet, the faith of these early Christians held strong. They frequently marched into their deaths singing hymns. They believed.

Questions for Thought

1. What do you chose to do when you are pelted with lemons: glorify the Lord, complain, or look for where Satan got a foothold?

2. If you choose to glorify the Lord, how do you go about it?

3. How do you follow in Christ's steps when you suffer?

4. How does Christ help you when you suffer?

5. Does your walk inspire others to follow Christ? Why or why not?

6. Do you feel separated from the love of Christ? Write a prayer about that, and if necessary, consult with your pastor.

CHAPTER 28

KEEPING THE COLOR AND FRESHNESS OF FAITH

Aside from their being a great way to add flavor to food you are preparing, you can use lemons for many other purposes. (Some of these I mentioned in other chapters.) For example, their high content of vitamin C provides the ascorbic acid needed to prevent the flesh of fruits from discoloring from the oxidization that occurs during air exposure. Lemon juice also is a meat tenderizer, and it replaces vinegar in dressings. In addition, lemon juice added to steamed vegetables will help them keep their bright colors and enhance their flavors.

I know that it seems odd to say *lemons*, *freshness*, and *faith* all in the same heading. But some companies do use "lemon fresh" to describe their products. So please stick with me. First, let's look at what the Bible has to say about freshness:

The meek shall obtain fresh joy in the LORD, and the poor among mankind shall exult in the Holy One of Israel.

—Isaiah 29:19 ESV

Does a spring pour forth from the same opening both fresh and salt water? Can a fig tree, my brothers, bear olives, or a grapevine produce figs? Neither can a salt pond yield fresh water.

—James 3:11–12 ESV

The Lord's joy is a daily joy and is refreshing, but we have to look for it daily and remember that the joy is there for the taking. How? I bet you know the answer. Spend time in the Word. I know I sound like a broken record; yet this is the only way to hear/read God's voice. We can refresh ourselves with His love. We can bathe ourselves in His sanctification. We can praise Him for what He has done for us. We can drink of the Spirit until we are more bubbly than the finest champagne. As we read His Word, we grow stronger spiritual "bones" so that "vitamin C" from the lemons can be absorbed to make us stronger. In the human body, "C" is needed to assist with healthy bones.

Water is a precious commodity in Israel; fresh water and salt water cannot flow from the same spring. Either the Spirit is with us or He is not. If we choose to be "fresh water," we present the message to others, perhaps in a new way. Alternatively, if we are "salt water," we must keep our spirits fresh and give flavor to our words, just as lemons give flavor to our salads and keeps them fresh. We have the responsibility not to "turn people off." It never pays to beat people over the head with the Bible.

It is important to choose our words carefully. We need to choose our words in a way that sets us apart. Again, be different, do not swear, and do not take God's name in vain. Do not gossip. That is a hard one; it is fun to talk about others. However, how would you feel if you were the person someone was talking about? If you get stuck gossiping, you can change the subject or say that is not like the "Jane" you know and end it there. If someone asks you why you are different, be prepared to give an answer. What are the answers?

Table of Answers[11]

Romans 3:24	We are declared not guilty of sin.
Romans 8:1	We will not be punished.
Romans 8:2	We have freedom from the law of sin that leads to death.
1 Corinthians 1:2	We are made holy and acceptable to Jesus Christ.
1 Corinthians 1:30	A judicial act of God wipes away our sins if we accept the work of His Son.
1 Corinthians 15:22	We will be made alive at the resurrection.
2 Corinthians 5:17	We are new people.
2 Corinthians 5:21	We receive God's righteousness. (See 1 Corinthians 1:30.)
Galatians 3:28	We are one in Christ with other believers.
Ephesians 1:3	We are blessed with every spiritual blessing in Christ.
Ephesians 1:4	We are holy and blameless.

Continued

Ephesians 1:5–6	We are adopted as God's children.
Ephesians 1:7	Our sins are gone; we are forgiven.
Ephesians 1:10–11	We will be under Jesus' authority.
Ephesians 1:13	We are identified as belonging to God by the Holy Spirit.
Ephesians 2:6	We have been raised up to sit with Christ in glory.
Ephesians 2:10	We are God's works of art.
Ephesians 2:13	We have been brought near to God.
Ephesians 3:6	We share in the promise of blessings through Christ.
Ephesians 3:12	We are able to enter God's presence with freedom and confidence.
Ephesians 5:29–30	We are Christ's body, the church.
Colossians 2:10	We are made complete in Christ.
Colossians 2:11	We are set free from our sinful nature.
2 Timothy 2:10	We will have eternal glory.

I have several favorite verses in that list—like those that say I am one of God's children, I have the ability to talk to Him freely, and I am considered a work of art, despite what I look like. These are important points to know and share. These points will "flavor" your interactions with people, because everyone is a child of God, whether they know it or not. These points will also influence your day-to-day reactions to situations.

> But grow in the grace and knowledge of our Lord and Savior Jesus Christ. Now what does the Bible say about salt?
>
> —2 Peter 3:18 NIV

> You are the salt of the earth, but if salt has lost its taste, how shall its saltiness be restored? It is no longer good for anything except to be thrown out and trampled under people's feet.
>
> —Matthew 5:13 ESV

> Let your speech always be gracious, seasoned with salt, so that you may know how you ought to answer each person.
>
> —Colossians 4:6 ESV

Hey! Paul wrote that second verse, and he was a fiery anti-Christian zealot, until he met Jesus. The changes the Lord can make in people are amazing. Paul kept his faith despite shipwrecks, imprisonments, starvation, and watching friends martyred. He also (most likely) wrote the book of Hebrews, which contains the "roll call of faith."[4] Reading that looks like the bright vegetables in a huge salad. We may have a little lemon juice as salad dressing in order to preserve the salad, but the same lemon juice preserves us as bright lights.

God is the preserving factor in our lives. Second Timothy 4:18 states, "The Lord will rescue me from every evil deed and bring me safely into his heavenly kingdom. To him be the glory forever and ever. Amen" (ESV). And 2 Corinthians 4:5–6 says, "For what we proclaim is not ourselves, but Jesus Christ as Lord, with ourselves as your servants for Jesus' sake. For God, who said, 'Let light shine out of darkness,' has shone in our hearts to give the light of the knowledge of the glory of God in the face of Jesus Christ" (ESV).

Questions for Thought

1. Are you feeling "lemon fresh" inside? Why or why not? How can you make it better?

2. It is hard to be a bright light when lemons are being hurled at you, but do you remember that science experiment at school with fruit? Most fruits have some acid in them and can conduct electricity. How can you shine a bright light today?

3. It is hard to remember to look for the Lord's joy. Journaling may help. Choose one of the scriptures above (or any other that inspires you), and make it your own. Put your name in it; personalize it. You are God's child.

4. Which of the verses in the Table of Answers touched you personally? Why?

CHAPTER 29

PURIFICATION

To scour stains from pots and pans, pour warm water into the vessel, add lemon slices, and let the contents simmer for about fifteen minutes, or until the food breaks loose from the pot. Lemons act as a purifying agent to cleanse the vessel.

I remember feeling despair so deep that I believed I had nothing left to offer God. What I forgot was that I do not have anything to offer Him in the first place, except myself. During this despairing period of my life, I experienced a time of deep purification. It was not pleasant, but I learned total reliance on Christ. I seem to relearn this lesson from time to time and at deeper levels because I never seem to "get" the whole thing God is trying to teach me.

Metals are more valuable when they are pure. Do you know that in order to get most pure metals, the ore must be melted into a liquid state first? Each metal has a melting point—a temperature at which it changes from a solid to a liquid. Here are some examples (all given in degrees Fahrenheit):

1. Copper—1,983
2. Gold—1,945
3. Iron—2,797
4. Nickel—2,647
5. Silver—1,760

6. Brass—1,660–1,710
7. Aluminum—1,220 (But it has to be electrified to exist.)

Note that all of the metals listed above, except for aluminum, were available during biblical times. Purified copper, gold, nickel, and silver were used as coins and in the making of valuable items, especially in the first tabernacle. (See Exodus 26 and 38.)

Alum is not the same as Aluminum. Alum, which is found in flakes near salt deposits, was discovered by Friedrich Wöhler in 1825. In 1889, Charles Martin Hall found a method that allowed for inexpensive manufacturing of pure alum. When the impurities were extracted, he also found that alum was an effective conductor of electricity, and if a current was passed through a nonmetallic conductor, the alum would separate. This was the discovery of aluminum.

Proverbs 8:10–11 (BBE) states, "Take my teaching, and not silver; get knowledge in place of the best gold. For wisdom is better than jewels, and all things which may be desired are nothing in comparison with her." All wisdom is in Christ. It is given to us to help us live godly lives. The fruit produced by godly wisdom is pure and helpful, especially during times of duress in the Christian's life. Matthew 7:16 says, "You can identify them by their fruit, that is, by the way they act. Can you pick grapes from thorn bushes, or figs from thistles?" (NLT).

Christ is in us, and we are in Him. I would say that is more precious than silver. We are called to have growing knowledge of God, the Spirit, His Son, truth, and sin. Riches, whatever type they are, do not mean much in the light of eternity. How we use riches to serve the Lord, yes, that matters.

But even riches do not protect people from the lemon press. Bad things happen, and those bad things can get very bad. Refer back to the melting points of those metals. My dear friends, there are times in our lives when we have to be taken to our melting points in order to be cleansed of impurities. Then we can be poured out into a new mold and receive a fresh start. Yes, it hurts, but the Lord is always with us. Once the process is over, we are stronger in our faith, wiser in our faith, and have more knowledge about how to serve Him. First Peter 1:7–8 explains, "So that the true metal of your faith, being of much greater value than gold (which, though it comes to an end, is tested by fire), may come to light in praise and glory and honour, at the revelation of Jesus Christ: To whom your love is given, though you have not seen him; and the faith which you have in him, though you do not see him now, gives you joy greater than words and full of glory" (BBE).

The refining process makes any impurities rise to the top so that the one working with the metal can skim them off. Our refining process, as uncomfortable as it is, prepares us to meet God and strengthens our faith. The process makes us more useful to God.

Satan may believe that he is throwing lemons at God's children, but in reality, Satan can only do what God allows him to do. Satan is not omniscient or all-powerful. Our focus needs to be on our responses. We need to stay faithful to the belief that God has our good in mind and plans our lives. We need to continue through the pain without giving into bitterness and despair. We need to be courageous. Jesus is our big brother, and He will carry us. He promised that He will never abandon us.

Questions for Thought

1. Describe a time when you were knocked down so hard you did not think you could get up again. How did you get back on your feet and your faith?

2. What sights just spontaneously make you want to worship?

3. Have you made a habit of really studying God's Word with a group? This is essential. Do not give up the devotion time, but also take time to get to know God in group studies. Talk to Him about this.

4. There are times when we feel as if we are being melted down to our core elements. What is the "metal of your faith"? What is the thing that "makes" you believe?

CHAPTER 30

THE WINDOW OF THE SOUL

Now we see a blurred image in a mirror. Then we will see very clearly. Now my knowledge is incomplete. Then I will have complete knowledge as God has complete knowledge of me.
—1 Corinthians 13:12 GW

Four tablespoons of lemon juice mixed with half a gallon of water makes an effective window cleaner. In the Old Testament, God used the word for *mirror* to describe visions from God given to His people. In the verse above, Paul is using the word as a metaphor. He is saying that what we will become, through the power of the Holy Spirit, is unknown to anyone but God.

Every day as I study, learn, live, and grow, my knowledge of God becomes more intimate. His knowledge of me is already complete. He knows the obstacles I must overcome that stand between us, blurring my image of Him. Through the Holy Spirit, Christ will teach me the truths and give me the spiritual knowledge I need so I can grow in Him.

Read what else Scripture says about growth:

But I thank God, who always leads us in victory because of Christ. Wherever we go, God uses us to make clear what it means to know Christ. It is like a fragrance that fills the air.
—2 Corinthians 2:14 GW

I pray that your love will overflow more and more, and that you will keep on growing in knowledge and understanding. For I want you to understand what really matters, so that you may live pure and blameless lives until the day of Christ's return.

—Philippians 1:9–10 NLT

Questions for Thought

1. What obstacles lay between you and full disclosure to Christ?

2. How do you see the Lord?

3. Are you comfortable with the thought that God has full knowledge of you? Why or why not?

4. Has your knowledge of God grown since you became one of His children? It is necessary to continue learning about Him. Do you understand why? (If not, find out.)

5. Through study of God's Word, you will become more like Jesus and more familiar with Scripture. You will learn history and, hopefully, will not be doomed to repeat it. You will form a close relationship with the Lord, which is something He desires. Is this something you desire?

CHAPTER 31

A DISCOLORED IMPLEMENT

To clean discolored utensils, use a cloth dipped in lemon juice, and then rinse the utensils with warm water.

In Hebrew, a tool can be a cutting instrument or a sword. *Tool* also can have some figurative applications, such as a hand, being able, drawing strength from, or yielding. It also can refer to words like *broaden, broken, consecrate, creditor, custody, debt, dominion, ministry, pain, power,* or *service.* Those are just a few of the applications. In Greek, *tool* translates as an offensive weapon.[10]

Isaiah 49:16–17 says, "I have engraved you on the palms of my hands. Your walls are always in my presence. Your children will hurry back" (GW). The context of this scripture is the capture of Jerusalem. In it, God is reassuring the people, through Isaiah, that He will not forget them. But He is chastising them like beloved children through their capture.

Some theologians believe that the walls the Lord refers to are the breached city walls. I believe that because Isaiah had warned the people so many times and was not heard, the walls could also be the ones around the people's hearts.

John 12:40 says, "He has made their eyes blind, and their hearts hard; for fear that they might see with their eyes and get knowledge with their hearts, and be changed, and I might make them well" (BBE). That was a fulfillment of a prophecy from Isaiah. One would think that the religious leaders—steeped in Scripture, having memorized it and spent days and weeks in the temple—would immediately recognize Jesus when He came. However, they had blind eyes because of greed, anger, and many other sins. They were tarnished so they missed Him. They were so accustomed to the way things were, so willing to accommodate Rome, and so afraid to give up their power that their hearts were coated with a thick tarnish. These men were Levites, the tribe that was to be serving God alone; yet, they served themselves. They knew the prophecies of the Scriptures better than anyone else did, but they could not see the fulfillment for themselves, much less the build-up on their hearts.

The religious leaders needed a thorough cleansing of the heart. They also needed a refresher course on their own religion, the tools to get close to God. The leaders lost their consecration (separate, belonging to God).[12] They did not yield to God; they made their own way. Their service to God was meaningless, offered by rote. Yet, God did not give up on His people.

Questions for Thought

1. What is the best Hebrew translation for *tool* in your life right now? Do you need to clean your "implement"? Do it.

2. Do you have walls up against people? Against God? I've been there. In some cases, I'm still there. Take a step of faith, and let the Lord in.

3. What do you think it means to be carved in the palms of God's hands?

4. Keep your eyes open for the Lord's moving in your life—please. Write about this.

PART SIX

GETTING DOWN AND DIRTY

CHAPTER 32

ALL DRIED OUT

For bleaching purposes, add 1/2 cup of lemon juice to your washer's rinse cycle and then hang your clothes outside to dry. The combination of the lemon juice and the sun will bleach your clothes.

Ezekiel 37:2–6 (MSG) reads, "He led me around and among them—a lot of bones! There were bones all over the plain—dry bones, bleached by the sun. He said to me, 'Son of man, can these bones live?' I said, 'Master God, only you know that.' He said to me, 'Prophesy over these bones: "Dry bones, listen to the Message of God!"' God, the Master, told the dry bones, 'Watch this: I'm bringing the breath of life to you and you'll come to life. I'll attach sinews to you, put meat on your bones, cover you with skin, and breathe life into you. You'll come alive and you'll realize that I am God!'"

Life sucks us dry sometimes. We are left with no energy, no desire, and no hope. One thing piles on top of another, and we feel buried and suffocated. We believe the water of Life can't reach us. Then we believe God has abandoned us; therefore, His Spirit is gone too. The problem is that we put God in a box. We think He can only do so much or that we shouldn't bother Him with our problems.

Ezekiel may have felt this way too. Babylon captured God's people. He allowed this because of their behavior. The Persians defeated Babylon and allowed the Israelites to return home, reasoning that Israel didn't need God to go home and had learned their lesson. Ezekiel then warned the Israelites that only God has the answers to life and only God can create life. Ezekiel knew that devotion to God would wane quickly.

After God told Ezekiel to prophecy over the bones, good old Ezekiel was obedient. He spoke to the bones just the way God told him to. (Come to think about it, I would not have told God "no" either.) I imagine Ezekiel's shock as the bones became complete skeletons, then the organs and tendons appeared, then the skin came on the bodies. But one thing was still missing: life.

Next, God directed Ezekiel to call the four winds to breathe life into the thousands of bodies, which lay in front of him. (Personally, I am impressed that Ezekiel was still standing.)

There were three points to this message that God gave Ezekiel: the first was that the captivity would end, the second was that God's people would have a second chance, and the third contained foreshadowing of the Messiah. The full story is in Ezekiel 37.

We have to realize that God is God. He is the Master. He holds life in His hands. When trials come, and they will, we need to go to our Father, our God. That's the key to successful travel through the trials.

Questions for Thought

1. What is sucking you dry right now? Are you talking to God about it on a regular basis? If not, start right now. Write it down.

2. What does having the "breath of life" brought to you mean to you personally? How has it changed you?

3. Can God be put in a box? Describe a time when you tried to cram Him into one.

CHAPTER 33

WINDOW CLEANING

As I mentioned in Chapter 30, four tablespoons of lemon juice mixed with half a gallon of water makes an effective window cleaner. *Cleansing* in Hebrew can mean ceremonial purification, moral purity, justification, righteousness, or being pardoned.

We can't get through life in a healthy state on our own. We can't be free from sin without Christ, we can't minister to others without being ministered to by Christ, and we cannot cleanse ourselves spiritually. Why do we forget that sometimes and think we can make it without Him?

Psalms 24:3–4 says, "Who may climb the mountain of the Lord? Who may stand in his holy place? Only those whose hands and hearts are pure, who do not worship idols and never tell lies" (NLT). Wow, that sounds like an impossible task. We all have our idols; let's be real. Our idols may be justifiable ones in our own eyes, but they are idols just the same. For example, getting ahead at work to increase our salaries to benefit our families sounds like a noble goal, but if it's done to the exclusion of getting ahead with God (through Bible study, prayer, and church attendance), our work has become an idol. If we are spending more time relaxing or keeping up with the next new trend rather than giving some of our time and finances to the Lord, then our time and money have become idols.

Are your hands and heart pure? What do you think about your spouse? Your co-workers? The person who just cut you off on the highway? Do you stretch the truth to make yourself look good? Do you cheat on your taxes? Are you cleansed in these areas, or are they still a bit dusty?

Another use of the word *pure* is in relation to refining metals by removing impurities. That sounds painful! However, as stated in a previous chapter, sometimes we need to go through uncomfortable and even fiery times so that God can remove the impure, ungodly parts that remain within us. In those times, we may be tempted to believe that God doesn't love us anymore or as much because our impurities are showing. Nothing could be further from the truth; God allows the heat of purification in our lives because He loves us too much to let us remain impure. Sometimes, He also allows hard times in our lives because He's punishing us. Hebrews 12:6 states, "For the Lord disciplines those he loves, and he punishes each one he accepts as his child" (NLT). And Proverbs 3:12 concurs. It states, "For the Lord corrects those he loves, just as a father corrects a child in whom he delights" (NLT).

If God didn't care, He wouldn't discipline us. God's discipline does not come from vengefulness; His discipline is out of love and for the purpose of our learning. Our God wants His children to remember their past, His promises, His fulfillment of those promises, and His love for us. Even though, like the Israelites, we consistently wander away, He will continue to consistently seek us out.

Just as God warned the Israelites, so today, God gives us warnings. And we, like the Israelites, are warned but still laugh at the "prophets"—those in our lives, like our pastors, parents, and teachers, who point out the errors of our ways.

Do you ever tell lies? Not even "white lies?" Do any of the following situations sound familiar?

1. Wife: "Does this dress make my backside look too big?"
    Husband: "Oh no, dear, you look great."
2. Friend: "Do you like this new recipe?"
    Other friend: "My goodness, yes. The taste is unique."
3. "I'm sorry I got home so late. The guys and I got to talking, and will you forgive me—again?"
4. "I didn't know I was speeding officer."

God never lies. That's reassuring to know. And His promises are just that: promises. He won't pull out a contract with fine print and point out some clause that nullifies a promise. That means a lot to me. I know that none of us is perfect, especially I am not, but God is. And it is He who cleans the windows to our souls. He sees who we are and loves us anyway because His Son died for us. All we have to do is believe. How simple!

Questions for Thought

1. What are your idols?

2. Are your hands and your heart pure? Why or why not?

3. Are you being disciplined by the Lord? Do you know why? If not, pray about it.

4. How do you feel about God being your Father?

5. What steps can you take to learn more about God and His promises? What promise will you choose to live by today?

6. Have you ever felt as though you were being cleansed by the Lord? How? Have you ever felt like you were being corrected by the Lord? What was that situation like? Write a prayer to Him about how you feel about those times now.

CHAPTER 34

LEMON VERBENA

Marilyn Scott O'Hara mentioned it several times to her daughter Scarlet. Her favorite plant was the lemon verbena. My only association with lemon verbena is that my grandmother wore it.

Lemon verbena is not part of the lemon fruit; it is an herb. It is used in sachets and as a flavoring, especially in bland foods. Lemon verbena compresses were said to reduce puffiness around the eyes, and adding it to vinegar was a way to soften skin. Once planted, lemon verbena comes back year after year. Our faith needs to be like lemon verbena, perpetual and distinctive. It has that distinct, lemony smell.

Thanks mainly to marketing, we associate the smell of lemons with cleanliness. However, sometimes that lemon smell may bring back memories of bitter times, like when my grandma used the lemon sachets to soothe her tears.

What we need to realize is that without flavor, without those times when we cry, and without those times when we need to roll up our sleeves and get our hands rough and dirty, we would still be spiritual babies. I can't share my faith without learning to do it and then actually doing it. I can't be an effective Christian for just an hour on Sundays. I can't be an authentic Christ follower without shedding some of my own tears and without reaching out to someone who needs help. I can't grow without going through hard times with the Lord, because that's when I learn the most about Him. Still, I know He is there; He said He would be. And like the sharp scent of verbena that permeates a garden or room, I feel Him helping me.

Questions for Thought

1. Instead of using "salt and light," I am using flavor and smell. Do you know why?

2. Find a scripture that refers to flavor.

3. What is the connection between getting our hands dirty and spiritual maturity?

4. Why do we need to cry sometimes? Who can we count on to soothe our tears?

5. Reflect on some times when you were distinctly aware of the Lord's presence. Write a description of what that felt like.

6. Sometimes, we need to soften our hearts. Pray today, and ask the Lord toward whom you need to soften your heart.

CHAPTER 35

DEGREASING

Did you know that a teaspoon of lemon juice added to your dishwashing detergent can help boost grease-cutting power? Our faith in Jesus Christ and His work on the cross functions much the same as lemon juice. It is similar to a math equation. (Do not worry, I am not a math wizard; that is my daughter.) Faith + Jesus' work + Knowing Scripture + Confession to Jesus = Justification. Do not let the big word scare you either. *Justification* means that it is just as if you have not sinned. You are clean.

Have you ever felt dirty, despite your confession to the Lord? I have. That's something Satan is particularly good at—making us feel guilty for confessed sin. Galatians 3:23–26 says, "Now before faith came, we were imprisoned and guarded under the law until faith would be revealed. Therefore, the law was our disciplinarian until Christ came, so that we might be justified by faith. But now that faith has come, we are no longer subject to a disciplinarian, for in Christ Jesus you are all children of God through faith" (NRSV). We are freed from sin by our faith in Christ's work.

Galatians 2:15–16 adds, "We ourselves are Jews by birth and not Gentile sinners; yet we know that a person is justified not by the works of the law but through faith in Jesus Christ. In addition, we have come to believe in Christ Jesus, so that we might be justified by faith in Christ, and not by doing the works of the law, because no one will be justified by the works of the law (NRSV).

Do you realize that your Christianity is *not* defined by doing good deeds? Yes, you should work out your faith and make it evident to all, but that is not what identifies you as a Christian. Your faith in Christ, regardless of what is going on in your life, identifies you as a Christian. No matter what Satan is whispering in your ear and no matter how you feel, remember that he is a liar and feelings aren't facts. You are justified, which means you are declared righteous because of Christ's work on the cross. Justification comes to us by faith alone.

Look at Hebrews 10:23: "Let us hold fast the confession of our hope without wavering, for he who Promised is faithful" (ESV). Jesus is faithful. He had multiple opportunities to turn away from what His Father wanted Him to do; yet, He fulfilled the prophet's prophecies. He confronted religiosity at the risk of His life, healed those who were considered "unclean," loved children, and confronted injustice. Jesus was a meek man, but He was not a weak man. He was a loving man who has earned our faith.

The author of Hebrews writes in chapter 4, verses 14–16, "Since then we have a great high priest who has passed through the heavens, Jesus, the Son of God, let us hold fast our confession. For we do not have a high priest who is unable to sympathize with our weaknesses, but one who in every respect has been tempted as we are, yet without sin. Let us then with confidence draw near to the throne of grace, that we may receive mercy and find grace to help in time of need" (ESV). Did you catch the "every respect?" He was socially isolated, and everyone wanted something from Him. His little band of twelve could be dolts. Huge crowds followed Him everywhere. He had to hide to pray. During His arrest and crucifixion, His disciples fled. He was beaten beyond recognition, His beard was pulled out, and I could go on. He experienced every temptation and pain, both emotional and physical, just like we do. Yet, through His willing sacrifice on the cross, we are freed from the grip of sin if we accept that work. That greasy scum, Satan the accuser of all Christians, can't stick to us anymore.

Questions for Thought

1. Have you ever done something, confessed it, and had it come up in your mind over and over again, making you wonder if you've really been forgiven? What was it? Write a prayer; then picture that problem nailed to the cross.

2. What identifies you as a Christian?

3. How has Jesus proven to you that He is faithful?

4. What does the thought that Jesus can sympathize with us in *every* circumstance mean to you?

CHAPTER 36

RUST REMOVAL

In order to remove rust, you can rub a lemon juice and baking soda paste onto chrome or copper, rinse, and then wipe/buff with a soft cloth or paper towel. We get rusty too and need to refresh our knowledge of the basics of our faith: Why do we need Jesus? Who is He? What did He teach, and how are we to apply it to our lives? Why do we need to fellowship? Why study the Word? Why be baptized? What is communion? I could go on, but I think you know what I mean. We need to be ready to answer questions, and we daily need to refresh/deepen our knowledge. It will also help us to avoid sin.

Copper was known to ancient civilizations, and the isle of Cyprus was famous for its rich supply. In large doses, copper is toxic. Yet, in biblical times, it was used to make bowls and coins, and the Israelites used it in the tabernacle and later in the temple. The Greeks used it for their armor. The Egyptians used copper to sterilize water and treat infections.

Chrome and copper have the tendency to rust and need to be polished in order to maintain their shine. In the same way, our lives can take on "rust" when we allow sin to enter in. The shine that should radiate from our lives is dulled.

One thing that dulls our shine is discord with another person. Matthew 5:25–26 says, "Make peace quickly with your opponent while you are on the way to court with him. Otherwise, he will hand you over to the judge. Then the judge will hand you over to an officer, who will throw you into prison. I can guarantee this truth: You will never get out until you pay every penny of your fine" (GW). As Christians, we are to shine with our different take on what society expects.

Brass, an alloy of copper and zinc, was discovered before 600 B.C. Brass can also rust and become dull. Zinc was discovered in 1746. It is used on any metal that may rust. Zinc is also used to make batteries.

First Corinthians 13:1 reads, "I may speak in the languages of humans and of angels. But if I don't have love, I am a loud gong or a clashing cymbal" (GW). Brass can be used to make instruments. My voice is an instrument that can be used to proclaim Christ. If my voice is tarnished by the sin in my life, the sound of it will be distorted, and my witness will be weak and unbelievable. I will sound like a clashing cymbal.

Numbers 21:4–9 says, "They set out from Mount Hor along the Red Sea Road, a detour around the land of Edom. The people became irritable and cross as they traveled. They spoke out against God and Moses: 'Why did you drag us out of Egypt to die in this godforsaken country? No decent food; no water—we can't stomach this stuff any longer.' Therefore, God sent poisonous snakes among the people; they bit them and many in Israel died. The people came to Moses and said, 'We sinned when we spoke out against God and you. Pray to God; ask him to take these snakes from us.' Moses prayed for the people. God said to Moses, 'Make a snake and put it on a flagpole: Whoever is bitten and looks at it will live.' So Moses made a snake of fiery copper and put it on top of a flagpole. Anyone bitten by a snake who then looked at the copper snake lived" (MSG).

We get rusty with our faith, just like the Israelites did. We sail along, going through the motions: church on Sundays, small group, ladies Bible study, and hopefully, a quiet time. We listen to the Christian radio station, send our kids to the Christian school, make sure they go to youth group, and watch our children's viewing/music habits. But where is our heart really? Do we do these things because we love the Lord and want to bring up the next generation to do the same? Or is it because it is expected of us? Where is our focus?

Questions for Thought

1. What is the state of the tabernacle of your heart?

2. What is the state of your spiritual armor?

3. Who/what are your opponents? What do you need to do to make peace?

4. Are you just going through the motions with your faith and grumbling along the way? Why?

5. Look up at the snake on the pole, what do you think it represents? (See John 3:14.)

CHAPTER 37

MOSQUITOES

It is said that lemongrass can be made into a paste to repel mosquitoes and that it works better than DEET. In our lives, we need a lemongrass paste, or armor, to repel the mosquitoes that attack us.

Ephesians 6:16 says, "In every situation take the shield of faith, and with it you will be able to extinguish all the flaming arrows of the evil one" (HCSB). Second Thessalonians 3:3 adds, "But the Lord is faithful; He will strengthen and guard you from the evil one" (HCSB).

It is hard to hold that shield of faith up high when Satan is focused on attacking you. Maybe this will help: Satan only attacks people who get in his way, so you must be doing something right for the kingdom if the enemy is concentrating on attacking you. However, be encouraged, because not only are you not alone in the battle (God is with you), but also there are more pieces of the armor at your disposal than just the shield.

Ephesians chapter 6 details the pieces of the armor. It instructs you, "Put on the full armor of God so that you can stand against the tactics of the Devil" (HCSB). Then the passage goes on to tell you to stand "with truth like a belt around your waist, righteousness like armor on your chest, and your feet sandaled with readiness for the gospel of peace." You are further instructed, "In every situation take the shield of faith, and with it you will be able to extinguish all the flaming arrows of the evil one. Take the helmet of salvation, and the sword of the Spirit, which is God's word. Pray at all times in the Spirit with every prayer and request, and stay alert in this with all perseverance and intercession for all the saints" (Ephesians 6:14–18 HCSB).

Whoa! This sounds like a lot to carry around all the time. However, it's important to remember that just like mosquitoes in the warmer weather, Satan hovers, buzzing around, waiting to sting you—but he is there whether the "weather" is hot or cold. Most of the time, mosquito stings aren't that big of a deal, but they are annoying. We scratch the bumps sometimes to the point of making them bleed and infected. Some mosquitoes even carry diseases like West Nile fever/virus, dengue fever, malaria, and various forms of encephalitis, to name a few. We have no problem with protecting ourselves against mosquito stings, so why should be balk at wearing the whole armor of God to ward off Satan's stings (which are far worse than mosquito stings)? What is it that you let get in the way when the "mosquitoes" start buzzing around? When do you lose your focus on the Lord?

Unlike mosquito repellant, the armor isn't a suit you go out and buy for yourself. This armor is supplied when you accept Christ as your Savior and He gives you the Holy Spirit as the seal of your salvation (Ephesians 1:13–14). The key is remembering to suit up. For example, you need to know what sin is, in order to avoid it. You cannot block the fiery darts of Satan's temptations if you don't know what you're up against is a temptation to sin. It is necessary to use the sword of the Spirit—the Word of God—to refute the enemy's attacks. Blocking the darts and refuting the attacks is your job, and that job can't be successfully carried out if you don't consciously put on your armor.

Sometimes we just need to dig in our heels and take a stand. It may be something as personal as, "I won't let this misfortune effect my walk with the Lord. In fact, I'll just get closer to Him." Or it may be witnessing to a lost friend. But we have to stand up for truth and not give up any ground, or we may end up running. (Don't feel bad; I've done that too.)

Let's look at the process of putting on our armor step by step. When Paul wrote Ephesians 6, his readers would have been familiar with armor because of the Romans, so we will look at their armor and how it relates to our armor.

A Roman soldier used a sturdy belt to hold his sword against his body. Everyone who saw him "girded" knew he was on active duty. That truth is the basis for everything that we do: as Christians, we should know that we are, like the Roman soldiers, *never* off-duty. In battle, our sword, the Word of God, should be as near to us as a Roman soldier's sword was to him.

1. Do you consider yourself off-duty in certain areas? Why?

2. Do you think you would be a more effective Christian if you remembered you are always "on duty"? Why ?

A soldier would also use his belt to gather up anything flowing and "gird his loins" so his actions weren't impeded. We too must use the belt of truth to tighten things up in our lives, draw in our wayward ways, and refute the devils lies so our actions in battle with the devil will not be impeded. We cannot let anything allow us to stumble in our walk with God or lose our focus on the Lord, especially during those times when we are being attacked.

Exodus 12:11 tells us about how the children of Israel were to dress as they ate the Passover meal: "Here is how you must eat it: you must be dressed for travel, your sandals on your feet, and your staff in your hand. You are to eat it in a hurry; it is the Lord's Passover" (HCSB). They were supposed to eat it with their loins girded. The loins were a vulnerable place. The flowing robes of the Israelites would impede their flight.

3. Where are you most vulnerable in your walk?

4. What holds you back from giving everything to the Lord? (I do not just mean money.)

5. Are there *lies* that you still trip over? (E.g., You are worthless.)

6. What is the truth?

The soldier's body armor was made of plates or bronze scales sown on leather, covering the front and sometimes the back. The Christians' protection is righteousness, procured for them in Jesus Christ. It is that fantastic grace. We don't have to fashion our armor or buy it or earn it. God has provided it through Christ; we just need to believe. First Thessalonians 5:8 says, "But since we belong to the day, we must be serious and put the armor of faith and love on our chests, and put on a helmet of the hope of salvation" (HCSB).

The soldier's breastplate stood upright when it was off. This is because most were connected at the shoulder. However, a soldier at war rarely took off his body armor. One never knew what would happen or when he would be called to serve. As Christians, we never can take off our body armor. We cannot choose when to be a Christian and when not to be. We are His all the time, period. As long as the armor is on, we are protected from those annoying "mosquitoes" of the devil's doings. The ancients believed that the conscience, bravery, and the psyche resided in the areas covered by the breastplate.

7. Do you consistently have the hope of salvation? Or do you think that something you have done is just too awful to be covered by the cross? Let me ask you something: What else could Christ have done to fix things for you? How much more torture would He have had to bear? There is no sin so big that His blood cannot cover it. Describe salvation and redemption in simple terms.

Faith is explained in Hebrews 11:1: "Now faith is the reality of what is hoped for, the proof of what is not seen" (HCSB). Faith, essentially, is trust. It is hard to trust in something or someone that we can't see, but we do it all the time. We have faith in gravity. We have faith in electricity. We have faith in the Internet. We can't see how this stuff works; it just does, and we rely on it.

Faith is also the result of teaching, what we've learned. Thank heavens this only applies to the Lord, because my brain isn't geared to physical science. Just ask my high school lab partner, Chuck! However, I have to choose to trust, and then I have to learn about what I am trusting in.

8. Do you trust the Lord when things get tough? Do you still trust the Lord when things don't work out the way you think they should?

Love is not part of the armor, but it is critical to our lives as believers in Jesus Christ. First John 4:19 says, "We love because He first loved us" (HCSB). Complete love reveals itself in the willingness to lay down lives for one another.

9. In the United States, we usually don't have to die to prove our love, but how willing are we to be inconvenienced? Will we go out of our way or step out of our comfort zones? Will we give some money to someone who needs it or at least buy a meal for someone who is asking for money?

We are called to love, and we need to risk being kicked in the shins and stepping on some hot places or tacks to do it.

Roman sandals, or more properly boots, covered the shins and soles of the foot. This not only protected their feet from unpaved ways but also from attacks that could cripple them. The feet and the legs are essential for walking and traveling, as well as for fighting in battle.

10. Are you willing to put "feet" to your love? How? Write an action plan here.

The helmet of a Roman soldier was the emblem of his country and the emblem of his status. As Christians, our helmet is salvation. We are covered by the blood of the Lamb; that is our emblem. Regardless of what happens to us or our status in this life, we can hold our heads up high because our heads are covered by the blood of the Lamb and we belong to Him.

11. How will you show that you belong to the Lamb? How can you do it in love?

The Roman sword was short in comparison to others swords. It gave them the advantage of stealth. It was also double-edged; one didn't have to worry about which edge was up. This doesn't just mean that we use the Word of God as a weapon to fight of the attacks of the Enemy, it also means that the Spirit of God, the power of God, if asked for, will lead us to understanding.

12. What does this mean to you?

After we put on our armor, we are told to pray at all times. I know, you are asking, *How can anyone pray all the time in this day and age?* Well, think of this, in Jesus' day, there were no appliances, no computers, and no real means of sanitation like we have today. Yet, He instructed people to pray at all times. Do you really think they were less busy than we are? Nope.

Praying at all times means having a running conversation with God throughout the day. If you notice something beautiful, praise Him for it immediately. When a prayer is answered, thank Him for it right away. If you need help, ask for it on the spot. God doesn't want to be slammed into a box, only to be taken out on Sunday mornings. He wants to be a part of our every moment.

In conclusion, we are told to stay alert. Where I live, we are told what to do during the summer to cut down on the mosquito population and avoid stings. Part of that is paying attention and using repellent to cover areas that are vulnerable to stings. As Christians, we need to be alert to our personal weak spots and to what Satan's up to in our lives.

Consider that, and list the things you think off here. Then ask God to help you maintain vigilance.

PART SEVEN

SOMETHING NEW

CHAPTER 38

THE SINK

Do you know that a paste of salt and lemon juice will clean and shine your sink *and* kill germs at the same time? Do you know why there are so many references to salt in the Bible? Salt was part of the offering to the Lord. Leviticus 2:13 directed the people, "Season every presentation of your Grain-Offering with salt. Do not leave the salt of the covenant with your God out of your Grain-Offerings. Present all your offerings with salt" (MSG).

Salt was an antiseptic, and it also symbolized hospitality, durability, fidelity, and purity. Salt strengthens newborn infants. The saying, "… to eat bread and salt together," or to season the offering with salt meant a sacred vow; it sealed a covenant. Meat rubbed with salt lasted in the desert heat.

In contrast, "salting" a person's land made it barren or referred to a barren land. After battle, the victor would sow salt on his enemy's land to starve them because salt inhibited plant growth.

Exposure to air causes salt to lose its savor or flavor. Salt is mined in the ground and from springs. In the New Testament, since salt preserved food, it was used as a metaphor for preserving people. It is also a metaphor for Christians, their grace, and sharing it among others. Colossians 4:6 advises, "Let your speech always be with grace, seasoned with salt, that you may know how you ought to answer each one" (NKJV). *The Message* translates this verse by saying, "Be gracious in your speech. The goal is to bring out the best in others in a conversation, not put them down, and not cut them out."

Salt and lemons are both associated with refining. Read Mark 9:48–50: "You're better off one-eyed and alive than exercising your twenty-twenty vision from inside the fire of hell. Everyone's going through a refining fire eventually, but you'll be well preserved, protected from the eternal flames. Be preservatives yourselves. Preserve the peace" (MSG).

Lemons are acidic and the acid will kill germs. Salt will clean the sink with an added boost of lemon without scratching it. A pleasing aroma remains. However, one is going to have to do some scrubbing to bring out the best in one's sink.

Are you going through the refining fire? It is hard to be the preservative when everything is falling apart around you. However, remember Mark 9:50 says, "You'll be well-preserved, protected from the eternal flames. Be preservatives yourselves. Preserve the peace."

Sink cleaning is not a glamorous job. Instead of whining, just do it. When you are getting scrubbed by the Holy Spirit, use the time to meditate or sing to yourself. That is how you preserve yourself, by welcoming the work of the Spirit within.

Questions for Thought

1. What is the connection between lemons and salt in your life?

2. How are you using salt (metaphorically) in your life? Are you making lands barren? Are you making food tasty?

3. Is your speech gracious or are you sour? Write a prayer about it.

4. Do you leave a pleasant aroma when you "clean the sink?" Why or why not? If not, how can you change that?

5. Will you be more aware of the "lemons" in life and use them to refine yourself? How?

CHAPTER 39

WHISTLING IN THE DARK

If you need to clean and deodorize your microwave, place 4 tablespoons of lemon juice in 1 cup of water in a microwaveable bowl and boil it for five minutes. The condensation from the boiled mixture will enable the microwave to be wiped clean easily. This process will also deodorize the oven.

Sometimes we need some freshening and deodorizing. First Peter 5:6–7 says, "So be content with who you are, and don't put on airs. God's strong hand is on you; he'll promote you at the right time. Live carefree before God; he is most careful with you" (MSG).

Psalm 19:13–14 states, "Clean the slate, God, so we can start the day fresh! Keep me from stupid sins, from thinking I can take over your work; then I can start this day sun-washed, scrubbed clean of the grime of sin. These are the words in my mouth; these are what I chew on and pray. Accept them when I place them on the morning altar, O God, my Altar-Rock, God, Priest-of-My-Altar" (MSG).

We all do stupid things and sin in stupid ways. We suffer from a variety of sins. For example, we covet in secret and subtle ways as we watch TV commercials, and we judge others as we listen to special music in church. In many ways, we are no better than the religious leaders of Jesus' time.

Sometimes we don't even realize the stupid ways in which we've blown it. It would be nice if we had some sort of referee following us with a whistle or something to alert us when we sin, or better yet, to warn us before we sin. However, life isn't like that.

We need to realign our thinking and be content. God knows where we are, and He knows who we are. We can't fool Him. We shouldn't try to fool anyone else either. God's hand is on us. Do you realize what an honor that is? Not only does our King know us, but also His hand is on us. In biblical times, that meant a blessing. Since God's hand is always on us, we are in the position of continual blessing. Why? Because His Son died for us. God is in control, and He is very careful with us.

God cleans the slate. Every time we repent, we start fresh. No one can step in for God, do His work, or know Him completely. But we can praise Him every day, recognize Him every day, and be amazed by Christ's work every day. Without the work of Christ, there would be no clean slate.

The Holy Spirit's work is to convict us (or nag at our consciences) of our sin. His other jobs are to pray for us, gift us, and allow us to communicate with our Father, to name a few. If we ignore the Spirit's conviction too many times, our consciences will become "seared." Hebrews 3:12–13 says, "See to it, brothers, that none of you has a sinful, unbelieving heart that turns away from the living God. But encourage one another daily, as long as it is called Today, so that none of you may be hardened by sin's deceitfulness." First Timothy 4:1–2 states, "The Spirit clearly says that in later times some will abandon the faith and follow deceiving spirits and things taught by demons. Such teachings come through hypocritical liars, whose consciences have been seared as with a hot iron."

Questions for Thought

1. Would you prefer to have a referee (like one from a basketball or football game) follow you around and blow a whistle every time you sin or are about to sin? Why or why not?

2. Why is it an honor to have God's hand on us?

3. What do you covet in secret? Write a prayer about it.

4. How do you feel about God being most careful with you?

5. Confession is part of gaining a clean slate. What things do you need to confess to God?

6. Look for opportunities every day to praise the Lord for who He is and what He has done for you. Write your first prayer of praise here.

THE FIREPLACE

Do you know that you can toss lemon rinds into the fireplace to freshen stale smells? I do not have a fireplace in my house, but the house I grew up in did. We used it on special occasions, like Christmas, New Year's Eve, and Thanksgiving. It was beautiful, with gold-lined glass doors set in bricks, and was in the living room, where we all gathered for those holidays.

As we would gather together as a family in front of that fireplace, the conversation would inevitably turn to memories of old times. We'd remember the funny things, the sad times, the special occasions—all the events that make a family special. And we'd remember who we were as a family and why we were so important to each other.

God would gather His people together from time to time too, recalling for them and reminding them of what made them special as His family. He even gathered them from exile. Deuteronomy 30:1–5 says, "And when all these things come upon you, the blessing and the curse, which I have set before you, and you call them to mind among all the nations where the Lord your God has driven you, and return to the Lord your God, you and your children, and obey his voice in all that I command you today, with all your heart and with all your soul, then the Lord your God will restore your fortunes and have compassion on you, and he will gather you again from all the peoples where the Lord your God has scattered you. If your outcasts are in the uttermost parts of heaven, from there the Lord your God will gather you, and from there he will take you. And the Lord your God will bring you into the land that your fathers possessed, that you may possess it" (ESV). And Psalm 50:5 says, "Gather My faithful ones to Me, those who made a covenant with Me by sacrifice." (HCSB)

Jeremiah 31:31–37 (NRSV) states (italics mine):

"The time is coming," declares the Lord, "when I will make a *new covenant* with the house of Israel and with the house of Judah. It will not be like *the covenant I made with their forefathers* when I took them by the hand to lead them out of Egypt, because they broke my covenant, though I was a husband to them," declares the Lord. "*This is the covenant I will make with the house of Israel after that time,*" declares the Lord. "I will put my law in their minds and write it on their hearts. I will be their God, and they will be my people. No longer will a man teach his neighbor, or a man his brother, saying, 'Know the Lord,' because they will all know me, from the least of them to the greatest," declares the Lord. "*For I will forgive their wickedness and will remember their sins no more.*" This is what the Lord says, he who appoints the sun to shine by day, who decrees the moon and stars to shine by night, who stirs up the sea so that its waves roar—the Lord Almighty is his name: "Only if these decrees vanish from my sight," declares the Lord, "will the descendants of Israel ever cease to be a nation before me." This is what the Lord says: "Only if the heavens above can be measured and the foundations of the earth below be searched out will I reject all the descendants of Israel because of all they have done," declares the Lord.

How many times did God confirm and renew His covenant with His people? Three times. They broke it *every* time. When the Israelites went overboard and worshiped other gods, or forgot who God was, they were disciplined, and then another promise was given. A good example is in Numbers 21:4–8:

But the people grew impatient on the way; they spoke against God and against Moses, and said, "Why have you brought us up out of Egypt to die in the desert? There is no bread! There is no water! And we detest this miserable food!" Then the Lord sent venomous snakes among them; they bit the people and many Israelites died. The people came to Moses and said, "We sinned when we spoke against the Lord and against you. Pray that the Lord will take the snakes away from us." So Moses prayed for the people. The Lord said to Moses, "Make a snake and put it up on a pole; anyone who is bitten can look at it and live."

Who sought out reconciliation and gave us a new covenant? God. Who provides despite our whining? God. We truly have a wonderful, loving Father God.

What does "covenant" mean? It is a promise. Sometimes it is bound on meeting some conditions, or sometimes it is unconditional (unbreakable). This idea is central throughout Scripture. We will finish this section with the old covenant and the new.

1. How do you feel about God consistently reaching out to His people?

2. Did God's people "deserve" being sought? Did they meet the conditions of the covenant?

3. What sacrifices are you making to get closer to the Lord? For example, are you getting up earlier to spend time with Him, learning to school your tongue, or changing your television- and movie-viewing habits?

4. Why did God send the snakes?

5. What did the pole with the snake on it portend (foreshadow)?

CHAPTER 41

CAN GARBAGE SMELL FRESH?

If you have a garbage disposal, it helps to throw in some lemon peel from time to time. The disposal will grind it up and leave the unit and sink smelling fresh.

We use the garbage disposal to get rid of food waste as we cook. We may throw in eggshells, peels, or bits and pieces of vegetables. Everything we dispose of comes from things we want, but we get rid of the parts that are useless to us. A garbage disposal has very sharp blades that mince the food waste into smaller pieces as water runs down the drain. The unwanted food parts are cut off and destroyed.

The Hebrew word *karat* means to be cut off. Several scriptures mention cutting off. Daniel speaks of this word (*karat*) when referring to the Messiah and His act of atonement. Daniel 9:26 (ESV) says, "And after the sixty-two weeks, an anointed one shall be cut off and shall have nothing. And the people of the prince who is to come shall destroy the city and the sanctuary. Its end shall come with a flood, and to the end, there shall be war. Desolations are decreed." This refers to Jesus' crucifixion for our sins. He was cut off from His Father during that time of darkness. Luke 23:44–45 (NLT) says, "By this time it was noon, and darkness fell across the whole land until three o'clock. The light from the sun was gone. And suddenly, the curtain in the sanctuary of the Temple was torn down the middle." The tear in the curtain signified the fact that Jesus' death on the cross provided us with direct access to God.

We cannot see the Lord. We cannot always feel His presence, but He has promised us that He will always be there, regardless of what we have done. We are His children. He may have to discipline us, but He is right there with us, helping us deal with the discipline if we ask Him to. Hebrews 12:6 explains, "For the Lord disciplines the one he loves, and chastises every son whom he receives" (ESV). Why? Because He is our heavenly Father. A loving human father keeps his children in line; why shouldn't our heavenly Father do the same? He is there to help and discipline, and He's also always there when we need to cry out to Him.

That garbage disposal illustrates the process of taking away the useless parts of our lives and grinding them up into compost. We throw the rind in there, the thing that protects us from "getting involved." Do you remember my description of the rind? It is thick. It is an attempt to protect ourselves. This can now go into the garbage disposal. The seeds of bad experiences or fear that keep us from sharing the gospel with the strength of Christ can follow the rind into the disposal.

We have been able to change what was meant for bad into good. The flowers from our lemon trees bloom with faith, and we've used the lemons to glorify God and help us grow in Him. Yes, the garbage disposal now smells wonderful, but we have to wonder, *What are we doing with our walk?* Does Jesus just intend for us to have our kitchen smell great?

Questions for Thought

1. What things do you want that you sense God is trying to "cut off" from your life? How are these things useful to you? If God wants them gone, how can you justify still holding onto them?

2. How was God's only Son "cut off?" Why did this happen? Find some verses to support your answer.

3. Describe a time when God heard your pleas for mercy or when you felt His presence in a special way.

4. Is your "garbage disposal" just making your kitchen smell great, or are you actually allowing our Father to "cut off" the bad parts of your life so He can use you more effectively? Where in your life do you see that occurring?

CHAPTER 42

PROMISES, PROMISES, PROMISES

We know that God's promises are true. He never goes back on His word. Jeremiah 33:14–16 states, "Watch for this: The time is coming—God's Decree—when I will keep the promise I made to the families of Israel and Judah. When that time comes, I will make a fresh and true shoot sprout from the David-Tree. He will run this country honestly and fairly. He will set things right. That's when Judah will be secure and Jerusalem live in safety. The motto for the city will be, 'God Has Set Things Right for Us'" (MSG).

Paul spoke of God's promises in Romans 9:3–5, which states, "If there were any way I could be cursed by the Messiah so they could be blessed by him, I'd do it in a minute. They're my family. I grew up with them. They had everything going for them—family, glory, covenants, revelation, worship, promises, to say nothing of being the race that produced the Messiah, the Christ, who is God over everything, always. Oh, yes!" (MSG). What Paul meant was that the Jews missed the arrival of the Messiah. This affected Paul so deeply that he would have changed places with all of them, if it were possible.

And what a marvelous plan we read about in Hebrews 8:7–13: "But we know the first was found wanting, because God said, Heads up! The days are coming when I'll set up a new plan for dealing with Israel and Judah. I'll throw out the old plan I set up with their ancestors when I led them by the hand out of Egypt. They didn't keep their part of the bargain, so I looked away and let it go. This new plan I'm making with Israel isn't going to be written on paper, isn't going to be chiseled in stone; This time I'm writing out the plan in them, carving it on the lining of their hearts. I'll be their God, they'll be my people. They won't go to school to learn about me, or buy a book called God in Five Easy Lessons. They'll all get to know me firsthand, the little and the big, the small and the great. They'll get to know me by being kindly forgiven, with the slate of their sins forever wiped clean. By coming up with a new plan, a new covenant between God and his people, God put the old plan on the shelf. And there it stays, gathering dust" (MSG).

God's people consistently found other gods to worship and added to the laws that He gave them. At times, they wanted to follow God to the point of excluding others, and at other times, they would forget about Him altogether. They even forgot to tithe, as though their provision came from their own abilities. Still, when their disobedience plunged them into trouble, they'd repent and cry out for help, and God repeatedly rescued them. Yes, like a loving father, He disciplined His children with captivity (a biblical sort of "go to your room") or destruction (a God-sized confiscation of all your toys), but they still would only turn to Him briefly, with rescue as their only real goal.

What motivated that relationship? Love. God was bound by His own covenant. He meant it when He said He loved the Israelites, and He means it when He says He loves you. Think about this: The Creator of everything craves a deep relationship with you. He promises never to leave or forsake you.

Your assignment is to find some of God's promises in the Bible that mean something to you personally. Keep a journal. Meditate on them. You will find them essential when the lemons come flying.

THE NEW COVENANT, PART ONE

The word *covenant* is used thirty times in the New Testament and is used in reference to both the old and new covenants.

First Corinthians 11:25–26 says, "In the same way, after supper he took the cup, saying, 'This cup is the new covenant in my blood; do this, whenever you drink it, in remembrance of me. For as often as you eat this bread and drink the cup, you proclaim the Lord's death until He comes.'" Luke 22:19–20 repeats this scene: "And He took bread, gave thanks, broke it, gave it to them, and said, 'This is My body, which is given for you. Do this in remembrance of Me.' In the same way He also took the cup after supper and said, 'This cup is the new covenant established by My blood; it is shed for you'" (HCSB).

Jesus shocked His disciples (something He was very good at) and interrupted the order of the Passover meal. Why? Because the ritual pointed to Him. Let's look a moment at The Feast of Unleavened Bread.

The Hebrew word translated *Passover* is *Pasach*, and it means "to step over." The special preparations for the Passover began on the evening of the thirteenth of Nisan, on which, according to the Jewish calendar, the fourteenth began; the day always was computed from evening to evening.

In preparation, all leaven had to be completely cleared out of the house. The head of the household searched for any that may have been missed and placed what he found in a special place while saying a prayer. The search itself was completed in silence.

Leaven or yeast causes bread to rise, but this rising takes time. Also, it just takes a little bit of leaven to spread through the whole loaf and affect it. In the Bible, leaven is an allegorical word for sin. Understandable, right? It just takes a little sin to spread through a whole body to affect it. So, unleavened cakes, which were cakes made without yeast, were to be the only breads used during the feast. These unleavened cakes could be made of wheat, barley, spelt, oats, and rye, but they were prepared before fermentation could begin. The symbolism is clear. The Jews eat only unleavened bread at this feast that commemorates the time when God rescued His people from their slavery. Now the eating of unleavened bread can also remind us of how God has rescued His people from their slavery to sin.

Hebrews 7:22 explains, "Jesus has also become the guarantee of a better covenant" (HCSB). He offered Himself as the Bread of Life, unleavened, because He knew no sin. When we take of Him, our sins are forgiven. Hallelujah!

Questions for Thought

1. How did Jesus replace the unleavened bread?

2. What did He say at the supper to foreshadow that?

3. Has the time of Communion during your church service become just a ritual? How can you fix that?

CHAPTER 44

THE NEW COVENANT, PART TWO

Exodus 12:4 speaks of using only an unblemished, pure lamb as a sacrifice. Later, this idea would point to Jesus, the sinless sacrifice atoning for our sins. Lambs used for sacrifices had to be whole, with no broken bones. When cooked, they could not be burnt; otherwise, something would have to be cut off. Families were to live with the animal and treat it almost as a pet for four days, so it probably would have been easy to become attached to a lamb.

At twilight (incidentally, about the time the Lord died), when there was still natural light, the whole assembly of the community was to slaughter the lambs they had in their homes. Imagine explaining this to your children. The noise. The stench of blood and feces. The pleading eyes of the lambs. Those little animals had not done anything but be themselves. They were innocent.

Jesus was innocent as well. He did not deserve having the flesh flayed off his back, being nailed to a cross naked, or being cut off from His Father. He did all of that for us. His eyes were full of understanding, love, and forgiveness right up until the very end, which is what challenges me the most.

Hebrews 7:24–27 says, "But because He remains forever, He holds His priesthood permanently. Therefore, He is always able to save those who come to God through Him, since He always lives to intercede for them. For this is the kind of high priest we need: holy, innocent, undefiled, separated from sinners, and exalted above the heavens. He does not need to offer sacrifices every day, as high priests do—first for their own sins, then for those of the people. He did this once for all when He offered Himself" (HCSB). And Isaiah 55:3 states, "Pay attention and come to Me; listen, so that you will live. I will make an everlasting covenant with you, the promises assured to David" (HCSB).

Jesus lives. He lives to talk to His Father about us. He understands because He has been here. I cannot fathom that love. Can you?

Questions for Thought

1. At any moment, Jesus could have called for an army of angels to rescue Him. Why didn't He, other than because it wasn't His Father's plan?

2. How did Jesus resemble the Paschal (Passover) Lamb?

THIS IS MY BLOOD

During the Passover meal, there were four official cups of wine given, with four traditional prayers, but again, Jesus broke the mold. I am sure the disciples did not know what to think. Jesus had gone completely off script! After all, they had never completely understood Him or His mission.

Jesus was expected to say the traditional Passover prayer over the first cup of wine, which began the official Passover meal. The prayer says:

> Blessed art Thou, Jehovah our God, who has created the fruit of the vine! Blessed art Thou, Jehovah our God King of the Universe, who hast chosen us from among all people, and exalted us from among all languages, and sanctified us with Thy commandments! And Thou hast given us, O Jehovah our God, in love, the solemn days for joy, and the festivals and appointed seasons for gladness; and this the day of the feast of unleavened bread, the season of our freedom, a holy convocation, the memorial of our departure from Egypt. For us hast Thou chosen; and us hast Thou sanctified from among all nations, and Thy holy festivals with joy and with gladness hast Thou caused us to inherit. Blessed art Thou, O Jehovah, who sanctifies Israel and the appointed seasons! Blessed art Thou, Jehovah, King of the Universe, who hast preserved us alive and sustained us and brought us to this season! [6]

The first cup of wine was the "Cup of Thanks." The wine was taken, and it was expected that everyone would then wash their hands.

However, from John's account of what happened when Jesus celebrated this last Passover with His disciples, we can see that the script wasn't followed as usual. John 13:2–18 (HCSB) reads:

Now by the time of supper, the Devil had already put it into the heart of Judas, Simon Iscariot's son, to betray Him. Jesus knew that the Father had given everything into His hands, that He had come from God, and that He was going back to God.

Next, He poured water into a basin and began to wash His disciples' feet and to dry them with the towel tied around Him. So He got up from supper, laid aside His robe, took a towel, and tied it around Himself. He came to Simon Peter, who asked Him, "Lord, are You going to wash my feet?"

Jesus answered him, "What I'm doing you don't understand now, but afterward you will know."

"You will never wash my feet—ever!" Peter said.

Jesus replied, "If I don't wash you, you have no part with Me."

Simon Peter said to Him, "Lord, not only my feet, but also my hands and my head."

"One who has bathed," Jesus told him, "doesn't need to wash anything except his feet, but he is completely clean. You are clean, but not all of you." For He knew who would betray Him. This is why He said, "You are not all clean." When Jesus had washed their feet and put on His robe, He reclined again and said to them, "Do you know what I have done for you? You call Me Teacher and Lord. This is well said, for I am. So if I, your Lord and Teacher, have washed your feet, you also ought to wash one another's feet. For I have given you an example that you also should do just as I have done for you. I assure you: A slave is not greater than his master, and a messenger is not greater than the one who sent him. If you know these things, you are blessed if you do them. I am not speaking about all of you; I know those I have chosen. But the Scripture must be fulfilled: The one who eats My bread has raised his heel against Me."

Once again, Jesus did not follow tradition; He exemplified humility. It was a common practice for people in general to provide water for their guests to wash their feet, and Jewish tradition had rigid rules for ceremonial hand washing. Yes, Jesus allowed the disciples to wash their hands, but He, the Servant of the Universe, washed their feet and rebuked those who were squeamish about it. Normally, only the lowliest of slaves washed people's feet.

During the traditional Passover meal, after the first cup, people dipped their hands in water, and this prayer was repeated: "Blessed art Thou, Jehovah our God, who hast sanctified us with Thy commandments, and hast enjoined us concerning the washing of our hands."[6] The traditional bitter herbs were presented to remind them of the bitter times in Egypt. Then the second cup of wine was filled, and the dishes were removed from the table.

Next, the youngest son, or child, was to ask, "Why is this night distinguished from all other nights? For on all other nights we eat leavened or unleavened bread, but on this night only unleavened bread? On all other nights, we eat any kind of herbs, but on this night only bitter herbs? On all other nights we eat meat roasted, stewed, or boiled, but on this night only roasted? On all other nights we dip (the herbs) only once, but on this night twice?"[6] (Most likely, John, being the youngest disciple, asked the question the family's youngest son or child would have asked.)

The father was then to go back through the Israelites' history to explain the significance of the Passover, beginning with Terah, Abraham's father, and including the idolatry, the story of Israel, the enslavement by Egypt, their deliverance, and the Law.

At this point, the dishes were returned to the table, and the Hallel was sung: "Blessed art Thou, Jehovah our God, King of the Universe, who hast redeemed us and redeemed our fathers from Egypt."[6]

Then the family again washed their hands, repeated the prayer, and then one of the two unleavened cakes was broken with thanks being given. At the Last Supper, this is the point at which Jesus gave the sop of bread to Judas.

Luke 22:20 recalls that when Jesus and His disciples celebrated this Passover meal, "He also took the cup after supper and said, 'This cup is the new covenant established by My blood; it is shed for you'" (HCSB). This was only the third cup of wine of the four that were to be drunk at this meal. But instead of having the fourth cup of wine, instead of finishing the ritual, the disciples went with Jesus to the Mount of Olives. Now, to very observant Jews, this would have been horrifying. But Jesus said that He was replacing that supper with His own and that covenant with His own blood, binding, something that Satan had no chance to fight against.

The disciples had been told countless times to remember what Jesus said to them. However, like a person feels when he or she gets stung with something like lemon juice in the eye, all they wanted to do was cry enough to get it out. The crucifixion was a huge sting. They couldn't see straight or think straight, until the unexpected happened: Jesus came back just as He said He would do. He returned just as it had been prophesied. And women, of all people, got to tell the disciples the news that they should have been anticipating! (Oh how I like that!)

Questions for Thought

1. Why was the Passover prayer so apt in this situation?

2. Why did Jesus wash His disciples' feet?

3. How can you exemplify this humility in your life?

4. Where does Jesus fit into the traditional Passover meal?

5. What does redeem mean? (Try looking up "relative redeemer.")

6. What did doing all this on the Paschal (Passover) night have to do with Jesus? Why couldn't He have chosen another night?

7. The third cup was another cup of blessing. What special blessing would you like to ask of the Lord?

8.   What special blessings have you received?

9.   What connections do you see between wine, the Passover, and Jesus?

CONCLUSION

I hope you enjoyed my unique look at trials in life. I pray that you answered the questions to the best of your ability and with prayer. I also pray that you learned some things along the way and that you've seen that keeping a journal is essential during growth spurts in a Christian's life. I've learned that the hard way.

Maybe you are one of the fortunate few who has avoided the lemons of life. You can still apply these little devotions to your life or to the lives of your friends.

To God be the glory!

—Ann

ENDNOTES

1. www.ancientegyptonline.co.uk/index.html accessed 9/1/12
2. E. Lowen, Main Minister at West Side Christian Church in Springfield, Illinois, live sermon on 5/20/12. Used with permission.
3. Bible Explorer McGarvey—MatthewMark Wordsearch. Corp 2007, McGarvey.
4. "Biography of D.L. Moody," http://www.believersweb.org (accessed 9/8/12).
5. "A Hymn and Its History: 'It Is Well with My Soul,'" http://biblestudycharts.com/A_Daily_Hymn.html (accessed 9/8/12).
6. The author of the book of Hebrews is in question. Many suggest Paul, Luke, Barnabas, Apollos, Silas, Philip, or Priscilla. See the notes in the *Life Application Bible*, copyright © 1988, 1989, 1990, 1991, 1993, 1996, 2004, 2007 by Tyndale House Foundation.
7. Ceil and Moishe Rosen, *Christ In the Passover* (Chicago, Illinois: Moody Press, 1978).
8. *The Holman Illustrated Bible Dictionary*, general editors Chad Brand, Charles Draper, and Archie England (Nashville, Tennessee: Holman Bible Publishers, copyright 2003, database © 2004 by WORDsearch Corp).
9. Adam Clarke, LL.D., F.S.A., etc., *Adam Clarke's Commentary,* database © 2004, WORDsearch Corp. (accessed 9/6/12).
10. James Strong, LL.D., S.T.D., *The Strongest Strong's Exhaustive Concordance of the Bible*, fully revised and corrected by John R. Kohlenberger III and James A. Swanson (Grand Rapids, Michigan: Zondervan, 2001).

11. *Life Application Study Bible* (Grand Rapids, Michigan: Zondervan, and Carol Stream, IL: Tyndale House Publishers, Inc., 2011).

12. *The Holman Illustrated Bible Dictionary*, general editors Chad Brad, Charles Draper, and Archie England (Nashville, Tennessee: Holman Bible Publishers, 2003).

WinePressPublishing
Great Books, Defined.

To order additional copies of this book call:
1-877-421-READ (7323)
or please visit our website at
www.WinePressbooks.com

If you enjoyed this quality custom-published book,
drop by our website for more books and information.

www.winepresspublishing.com
"Your partner in custom publishing."

CPSIA information can be obtained at www.ICGtesting.com
Printed in the USA
LVOW11s0232150713

342697LV00005B/15/P